YOU'RE A TEACHER NOW!

What's Next?

TOM HIERCK   ALEX KAJITANI

Solution Tree | Press   *a division of*
Solution Tree

555 North Morton Street
Bloomington, IN 47404
800.733.6786 (toll free) / 812.336.7700
FAX: 812.336.7790

email: info@SolutionTree.com
SolutionTree.com

Visit **go.SolutionTree.com/teacherefficacy** to download the free reproducibles in this book.

Printed in the United States of America

Library of Congress Cataloging-in-Publication Data

Names: Hierck, Tom, 1960- author. | Kajitani, Alex, author.

Title: You're a teacher now! What's next? / Tom Hierck, Alex Kajitani.

Other titles: You are a teacher now! What is next?

Description: Bloomington, IN : Solution Tree Press, [2024] | Includes
    bibliographical references and index.

Identifiers: LCCN 2023043524 (print) | LCCN 2023043525 (ebook) | ISBN
    9781958590553 (paperback) | ISBN 9781958590560 (ebook)

Subjects: LCSH: Teaching--United States. | Effective teaching--Methodology.

Classification: LCC LB1025.3 .H537 2024 (print) | LCC LB1025.3 (ebook) |
    DDC 371.1020973--dc23/eng/20231106

LC record available at https://lccn.loc.gov/2023043524

LC ebook record available at https://lccn.loc.gov/2023043525

Solution Tree
Jeffrey C. Jones, CEO
Edmund M. Ackerman, President

Solution Tree Press
President and Publisher: Douglas M. Rife
Associate Publishers: Todd Brakke and Kendra Slayton
Editorial Director: Laurel Hecker
Art Director: Rian Anderson
Copy Chief: Jessi Finn
Senior Production Editor: Tonya Maddox Cupp
Proofreader: Mark Hain
Text and Cover Designer: Rian Anderson
Acquisitions Editor: Hilary Goff
Assistant Acquisitions Editor: Elijah Oates
Content Development Specialist: Amy Rubenstein
Associate Editor: Sarah Ludwig
Editorial Assistant: Anne Marie Watkins

DEDICATION

We who were once new teachers ourselves often look back on those beginning years as a time of great stress and overwhelm. Eventually, we found our way, thanks to the willingness of others to take time they had little of, share experience they had much of, and encourage us to hang in there, often one week, one day, or even one class at a time.

This book is dedicated to all those people who supported us as new teachers and who continue to support new teachers every day, in myriad ways . . . .

The colleague in the next room over. The administrator in the office down the hall. The mentor teachers, coaches, and support providers. The loved ones with us on this journey. The students and their parents and guardians who have found themselves on the roster and in the classroom of a new teacher. We thank each and every one of you for supporting new teachers, welcoming them, and understanding that the greatest investment that we can make in our collective future is to provide students with highly effective, happy teachers for many years to come.

We dedicate this book to you.

With gratitude,
Tom Hierck and Alex Kajitani

ACKNOWLEDGMENTS

Although only two names appear on the cover, this book would not be possible without the support and input of many colleagues and friends.

Beginning with our Solution Tree family, we would like to thank the following key supporters: Claudia Wheatley, who first had the idea that the two authors would make a good partnership and produce a bestselling book for those educators who are new to their role; Jeff Jones, who built a company that encourages educators to find their voice and share that with colleagues; Douglas Rife, the president and publisher of Solution Tree Press, who provided us with the opportunity and encouragement to develop and write the book; Tonya Cupp, our senior editor, who helped refine the rough manuscript into a book that flows and makes sense for busy teachers; Mark Hain, our proofreader; Rian Anderson, our cover and text designer, who created the colorful and engaging cover that conveys the central message of the book; and Shik Love and Kelly Rockhill, whose skills in marketing and promotion will ensure this book reaches a wide audience and can have the maximum benefit to colleagues.

Additional members of the Solution Tree team who worked diligently to support our work and refine the content include Sarah Payne-Mills, director of corporate communications; Amy Rubenstein, content development specialist; and Kendra Slayton, associate publisher.

We would also like to acknowledge the following novice teachers who met with the authors to share some insights and concerns that helped to shape the conversational tone of the book.

Samar Ahmed	Matthew Lyon
Lina Al-Saati	Amy McCleary
Sarah Barbuto	Farida Nurgat
Julia Farronato	Katelyn Scott
Lauren Gray	Tyler Szczucki
Asima Iqbal	Emily Swica
Jasmine Johal	Lauren Woolley

We are confident they will make valuable contributions to the Halton District School Board in Burlington, Ontario, Canada, where they have begun their teaching careers. Thanks also to our colleague Peter Marshall for coordinating the meeting with the group.

Solution Tree Press would like to thank the following reviewers:

Courtney Burdick
Apprenticeship Mentor Teacher
Spradling Elementary—
Fort Smith Public Schools
Fort Smith, Arkansas

Hallie Edgerly
Eighth-Grade Science Teacher and
Instructional Coach
Adel-DeSoto-Minburn Middle School
Adel, Iowa

Rachel Jorgensen
Special Educator
Anoka High School
Anoka, Minnesota

Louis Lim
Principal
Bur Oak Secondary School
Markham, Ontario, Canada

Paula Mathews
STEM Instructional Coach
Dripping Springs ISD
Dripping Springs, Texas

Christie Shealy
Director of Testing and Accountability
Anderson School District One
Williamston, South Carolina

Visit **go.SolutionTree.com/teacherefficacy** to download the free reproducibles in this book.

TABLE OF CONTENTS

About the Authors. xi

Introduction 1

CHAPTER 1
How Do I Set Up My Classroom? 3

Ensure Everything or Everyone Is Safe, Clean, and Seen 3

Use a Seating Chart 8

Think About What to Put On the Walls. 9

Plan for Where to Place Classroom Materials and Supplies 11

Final Thoughts: Ideas Are Everywhere 15

CHAPTER 2
How Can I Build Relationships With Students? 17

Pronounce Students' Names Correctly 18

Know Students' DNA 19

Use What You Know to Build Connections and
Further Learning 21

Say "Hello" 21

Say "Goodbye". 22

Know a Bit About Students' Living Situation 22

Tell a Story 24

Show Your Stuff 25

Just Ask. 25

Be Real 26

Remember the Hidden Relationships That Exist
in the Classroom 28

Build Students' Relationship With the Content 28

Help Students Build Relationships With Each Other 28

Final Thoughts: The Moments That Matter. 29

CHAPTER 3
How Should I Manage My Classroom?
How Should I Manage My Classroom? 31

Accept That Imposter Syndrome Is Totally Normal 32

Determine Necessary Classroom Procedures and Routines . . . 33

Teach Classroom Procedures and Routines to Students 38

Project Confidence. 41

Final Thoughts: Everything Matters. 43

CHAPTER 4
How Do I Get Students to Behave?
How Do I Get Students to Behave? 45

Promote Appropriate Behaviors 46

Discourage Inappropriate Behaviors 51

Final Thoughts: That One Student 56

CHAPTER 5
How Do I Plan and Deliver Engaging Lessons?
How Do I Plan and Deliver Engaging Lessons? 57

Understand Where Engagement Starts 58

Know the Elements of an Engaging Lesson 58

Plan for How to Wrap Things Up 66

Final Thoughts: Evolve, Improve, and Stay Flexible 67

CHAPTER 6
How Do I Know When Students Have Learned?
How Do I Know When Students Have Learned? 69

Understand the Purpose of Formative Assessment. 69

Understand the Purpose of Summative Assessment and
Student Mastery 71

Understand the Purpose of Grading 73

Offer Second Chances 75

Plan Interventions Driven by Evidence 77

Final Thoughts: Mastery and Outcomes 79

CHAPTER 7

How Do I Work With Parents and Guardians? 81

Remember That *Parent*, *Guardian*, and *Family* Can Mean
Different Things 82

Find Parents' and Guardians' Preferred Method of Contact . . . 82

Use the Power of Questioning 84

Invite Parents and Guardians In 89

Final Thoughts: Working Together 91

CHAPTER 8

How Do I Take Care of Myself? 93

Understand Your Self-Care Options 94

Take Time For Yourself 95

Foster Relationships and Connectedness 96

Manage Your Secondary Traumatic Stress 99

Recognize and Control Your Emotions 102

Final Thoughts: Plan Your Self-Care 104

EPILOGUE

Building a Long-Term Career as an Educator 105

Define (or Redefine) What Success Looks Like 106

Deal With the Money Part of Teaching 106

Build Your Network 106

Surround Yourself With Good People 107

Invest in Yourself and Your Professional Learning 107

Be Reflective 108

When We Teach, We Live Forever 109

References and Resources 111

Index 119

ABOUT THE AUTHORS

Tom Hierck has been an educator since 1983 in a career that has spanned all grade levels and many roles in public education. His experiences as a teacher, an administrator, a district leader, a department of education project leader, and an executive director have provided a unique context for his education philosophy.

Tom is a compelling presenter, infusing his message of hope with strategies culled from the real world. He understands that educators face unprecedented challenges and knows which strategies will best serve learning communities. Tom has presented to schools and districts across North America with a message of celebration for educators seeking to make a difference in the lives of students. His dynamic presentations explore the importance of positive learning environments and the role of assessment in improving student learning. His belief that every student is a success story waiting to be told has led him to work with teachers and administrators to create positive school cultures and build effective relationships that facilitate learning for all students.

His most recent works include *Trauma-Sensitive Instruction: Creating a Safe and Predictable Classroom Environment* and *Trauma-Sensitive Leadership: Creating a Safe and Predictable School Environment* (both with John Eller).

In 2003, **Alex Kajitani** was a struggling new teacher in one of California's poorest neighborhoods. His middle school students seemed unmotivated, unengaged, and uninterested in the mathematics he was teaching. Demoralized and desperate, he set out on a journey to turn his class—and his life—around.

Today, Alex holds the title of California Teacher of the Year and was a top-four finalist for National Teacher of the Year. He is lauded for his innovation and real talk as a teacher and leader and is also known around the world as *The Rappin' Mathematician*.

Alex's journey from frustrated new teacher to White House honoree is one he now shares with educators across the country. He tells refreshingly honest stories of what it truly means to connect with students and colleagues and interweaves these stories with proven strategies that educators can implement the very next day to make an immediate impact.

A highly sought-after speaker and a top authority on engaging students, relationship building, and teacher leadership, Alex is the author of several books, including *Owning It: Proven Strategies to Ace and Embrace Teaching*, which was named Recommended Reading by the U.S. Department of Education. He is also an expert on teaching online; he is the author of *101 Tips for Teaching Online*, and his virtual programs and videos are used around the world. Alex has a popular TED Talk and was featured on *CBS Evening News*, where Katie Couric exclaimed, "I *love* that guy!" And you will, too!

To book Tom Hierck or Alex Kajitani for professional development, contact pd@ SolutionTree.com.

INTRODUCTION

There are a lot of paths to becoming a teacher. Some dream about it from an early age and get as much practice as they can en route to earning a teaching credential and, eventually, that dream job. Others seemingly fall into the job, having worked various other jobs throughout their lives, only to find they're willing to "give teaching a shot" after a friend, family member, or some experience suggests they try it. Still others take the job, perhaps with some reluctance, when the life they are living takes a turn, and teaching seems a good option given the circumstances.

Regardless of how you came to this profession (and ultimately this book), anyone who has ever held the noble title of *teacher* has had that initial moment where they ask themselves, "What have I got myself into?"

Those moments are followed by subsequent, periodic moments of asking oneself the following questions.

- "Is this the right profession for me?"
- "Am I making a difference?"
- "How can I do this better?"

The book you are about to read isn't going to eliminate these questions from your mind; however, it will provide some answers and avenues to explore so you can be highly effective—as a new teacher or in the new educator role you've taken on.

As the authors of this book, we bring over sixty-five years of combined educational experience across a variety of roles and contexts, and we have worked and interacted with tens of thousands of educators across the United States and Canada. Our hope is that reading this book feels more like a casual conversation over coffee, where you can imagine being in the room with other like-minded colleagues exploring the issues, frustrations, and successes that are all a part of this wonderful profession.

If you've arrived at this profession after having worked in another sector, this book shows you how to incorporate the skills you've already built and the experience you've accumulated into a new set of skills and experiences, all while working with students. If you've arrived at this profession with limited training (perhaps you were thrown into it without much training), this book gives you a solid look into the most critical aspects of teaching and will get you thinking, walking, and talking like a well-trained teacher. However, and from wherever you've come to this profession and this book, we hope the title inspires and empowers you—because, you're a teacher now. What's next?

In classrooms everywhere, teachers are busy teaching. But in each of those classrooms, a multitude of things are happening. While some teachers are commanding the classroom with confidence, others are struggling to simply hold their students' attention for a short period of time. While some are leading their students through engaging activities and thought-provoking discussions, others are pleading for their students to simply quiet down so that they can give directions. And while some students are walking into classrooms that are welcoming and bright, others are walking into classrooms that might not be as effective or inviting as they could be.

So, the "what's next" is reading through this book with a fierce determination to be the type of teacher that you always wish you'd had when you were in school. Or perhaps the type of teacher that you did have and now want to emulate. You can do it, through a series of ideas, strategies, and experience relayed by other teachers, as well as—to be honest—mistake making along the way. It is our hope that this book helps minimize those mistakes.

In chapters 1 and 2, we help guide you through how to set up your classroom for success and turn it into a space where students feel safe, which is critical to learning. In addition to helping you set up this space, we provide guidance about how to manage your classroom and students, so you stress less and teach more.

Chapters 3 and 4 hit at the heart and soul of teaching, as they give you practical, immediately implementable strategies that you can use to build relationships with your students, especially those who behave in unexpected and challenging ways.

Throughout chapters 5 and 6, we share straightforward advice on how to plan lessons that are engaging, meaningful, and fun to teach, as well as how to recognize when students are learning, when they aren't, and what to do in both situations. Of course, many students come to us with unique needs and challenges, and so we cover how to help all students learn.

Finally, chapters 7 and 8, along with the epilogue, give you real strategies and ideas on how to proactively address the parts of being a teacher that many don't see but are essential to success: how to work with your students' parents and guardians; how to take care of yourself and stay balanced in a profession that has a seemingly insatiable hunger for all of your time; and how you can build a career that is fulfilling and meaningful.

Throughout the book, you'll find Tips to Thrive that highlight ideas and strategies from real teachers who, like you, are doing the work each day. They've tried and retried what they've shared (and made plenty of mistakes along the way), and you can benefit from their wisdom. The tips are thoughtfully placed in each chapter so you can walk away with ideas that you can implement immediately in your own classroom.

Every educator arrives at this role with a desire to make a true difference. You are not apt to have the desire to chronicle *what is*, but, instead, to help your students imagine (and sometimes reimagine) *what could be*. Remember the person you presented yourself as in your job interview? That's the person you truly believe you are, the person your school most needs, and the person who will make a true difference in your students' lives!

Welcome to teaching.

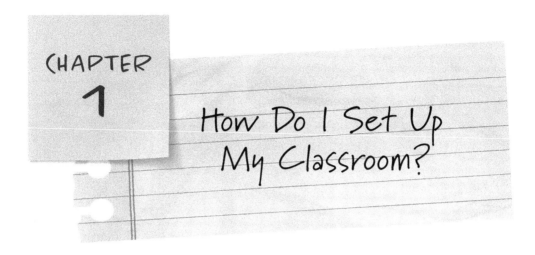

CHAPTER 1

How Do I Set Up My Classroom?

Think about walking into your favorite restaurant. Or maybe it's a coffee shop. Why do you love it so much? Sure, the food is great, but most likely, there's more to it. Perhaps you like the way the tables are arranged or the artwork on the walls. Maybe the staff greet you enthusiastically when you walk in, and the service is friendly. Hopefully, the place is clean. (Does *anybody* feel comfortable in a restaurant with a filthy bathroom?)

Your classroom is a combination of the social, emotional, and learning components your students need (and even crave). You can view it this way: "many aspects of your classroom environment can affect student motivation and that students who are more motivated, put more effort into learning activities" (Ambrose, Bridges, Lovett, DiPietro, & Norman, 2010, p. 74). In fact, several studies show that "students' classroom learning environment perceptions were found to be one of the significant predictors for students' academic achievement" (Hafızoğlu & Yerdelen, 2019, p. 251).

So, the way you organize your classroom is important. In this chapter, we address the following topics so that you can build a warm and inclusive classroom where students feel like they belong and can do their best work.

- Ensure everything or everyone is safe, clean, and seen.
- Use a seating chart.
- Think about what to put on the walls.
- Plan for where to get classroom materials and supplies.

Before we get into the nitty-gritty of setting up your classroom, stop and ask yourself, "How do I want students to feel when they walk in?" At the minimum, students need that coffee-shop feeling—they need to feel safe and seen and that the room is clean.

Ensure Everything or Everyone Is Safe, Clean, and Seen

Have you ever been on an airplane reading a book when you hit major turbulence and the plane starts to shake and career? Suddenly, it becomes difficult to read that book. What's changed?

You no longer feel safe.

Ever walk into a restaurant and, as you go to the counter to place your order, notice that the place is a mess? Perhaps there are food scraps that haven't been cleaned up or the trash bin is overflowing. Suddenly, you get this sinking feeling that the food you're about to order might not sit well in your stomach. What's changed?

You realize the place isn't clean, and you no longer want to be there.

Or, have you ever been excited to go to a party, but when you get there, nobody talks to you? Now, instead of being excited, you stand in the corner, looking for the nearest exit. What's changed?

You don't feel seen.

How we set up our classroom plays an important role in how students feel, and ultimately, how much they learn while they are in our classrooms. From the moment they walk in to the moment they leave (and every moment in between), they need to be in an atmosphere where they're seen, and where things are safe and clean.

Make It Safe

Because your goal as a teacher is to ensure learning for all students, the elements of safety, visibility, and cleanliness are necessities before learning can occur (Thomas B. Fordham Institute, 2021). Feeling safe and valued is vital to a student's development. Second only to physiological needs, Abraham Maslow's (1943) hierarchy of needs cites safety as one of the most important and critical needs that must be attained to live a fulfilling life. Learning suffers when students fear for their safety, worry about being bullied, or don't sense their teachers have high expectations for their success.

In reflecting on how to make your classroom safe, it's important to also consider what factors might make students feel unsafe, both in the classroom and in school generally. Consider, for example, the many sources of uncertainty and anxiety this generation of students is facing, ranging from bullying, gun-related violence and lockdowns, and the global pandemic shutdown and fallout to a world where everything feels like it's being recorded, measured, and judged, with the smallest mistakes leading to significant personal and social consequences. For teachers and students alike, it can be hard to find a place to take a deep breath and get to learning and growing. It's impossible to do this if you're not feeling safe.

Much as you cannot protect students from every fear the world throws at them, do think about what you can do to set up your classroom in a way that keeps safety at the forefront of your priorities. Do this by setting up a classroom where students can easily do the following.

- Get from the classroom door to their seat
- Get from their seats to the exit
- Move around the room without bumping into or tripping over things—especially other students.

Being prepared for school shootings is a sad but true reality that teachers must incorporate into their safety plans and consider when setting up their classrooms. Know your school's layout and where your classroom is in relation to the building in general. Practice opening and locking your classroom windows as well as locking and barricading your door. In addition, make sure students can move quickly and efficiently through and around their desks when needed.

We get into this more deeply when we talk about arranging desks in the following section.

Keep It Clean

Don't worry about setting up the perfect classroom. We'll talk more about what to do with your walls in the next section, but for the moment, know that your walls don't need to be adorned with inspiring posters or amazing artwork—and you don't have to be that social media superstar teacher who is always showing off the latest upgrade. Just make sure your room is clean, both in terms of hygiene and efficiency. As the year goes on, you'll find plenty of things you can put on your walls and place on your shelves.

So what makes for an efficient classroom? It sounds simple, but make sure trash goes directly in the trash can. In fact, ensuring you have enough trash cans for your room will go a long way. If you only have one, consider putting it near the door so students can throw things away on their way into and out of your classroom. If there's one thing we learned to do during the COVID-19 pandemic, it's to wipe down the desks and other surfaces each day. Your school might already have cleaning requirements in place. Find out who is expected to perform these procedures (for example, you, you and your students, or custodial staff).

The tougher part is that a clean room also means ensuring things like lights, heaters, and door locks function properly and that anything that is damaged gets repaired. One of the most important staff members to know on campus is your school's custodian. Not only can this person get repairs made as quickly as possible, but custodians also know where extra desks, chairs, and much-needed supplies are. Of course, like teachers, most custodians are also crazy busy, so here are simple ways to build a meaningful relationship with them.

- **Introduce yourself:** When you see them on campus, simply introduce yourself: "Hi, I'm Glenda. I just started in room 211, and I really wanted to meet you." Find out the best way to get hold of them. Some prefer email, but others prefer you just stop by their office.

- **Say "Hello":** Whenever you see them, simply say, "Hello." Being a school custodian can often be a lonely job, as there may be just one of them per campus, so a simple greeting helps them feel seen and included.

- **Say "Thanks":** Replacing a desk, making a repair, or vacuuming a carpet might be part of their job description, but it often goes unnoticed and unappreciated. You don't need to send them a gift card or bake a fresh batch of cookies—although who wouldn't love that? Verbal praise also ultimately raises a person's commitment to a job, so even a simple *thank you* has a profound impact and goes a long way in helping keep your room in order (Zhao, Yang, Han, & Zhang, 2022).

Be Seen

From the moment they enter your classroom to the moment they exit, you should be able to see your students, and they should be able to see you. This means setting up your classroom in a way that nobody's view is obstructed and everyone is in your view.

The catch with making decisions about how to arrange desks is that most of the time, you won't have a choice in the type of desks or chairs that populate your classroom. Whatever is in there is most likely the result of a large purchase your school or district made, so the good news is there might be extras when something needs to be replaced. What you do have control over is how they are arranged. If you're in a room (such as a theater or science lab) where the seats are already permanent, remember that you can choose where each student sits.

Ultimately, the goal is to arrange your desks in a way that everyone is facing the front of the classroom, and you can see everyone's faces. Nobody should have to turn their head more than 90 degrees to see the front of the classroom, and nobody should have to rotate their chair. When students can easily see what's happening, they are much less likely to get distracted and much more likely to stay engaged. At the same time, being able to see all of your students' faces also helps you monitor how engaged your students are. As the school year progresses, you'll get really good at reading your students' facial expressions, and you'll be able to identify which students are engaged and which are confused, responding accordingly to each.

Here are some additional tips for arranging your desks for maximum success, no matter what grade or subject you teach.

- Make sure you can easily walk to all sides of your classroom.
- Make sure you can see every student's face from the front of the classroom, and that everyone in the class can see you.
- Create space for stuff. You can, in one way, consider your room an airplane. Ask students to stow items below their seats.
- Consider putting your desk at the back of the room or at least off to the side. This opens up much-needed space at the front of the classroom and helps you remember to move around the room instead of sitting at your desk.
- Remember that it doesn't need to be forever. If it's not working, you can change it. There is no single perfect way to arrange your desks. You can get more creative as the year—and years—go on. But for now, arrange them in a way where everyone is safe and seen.

Keep it simple.

Tips to Thrive

A few days before school starts (or, if the school year has already started, do this whenever possible), walk around your campus and pop into some of the other classrooms to see how the desks are arranged. This allows you, potentially, to see several options before deciding on your own, and it's also a great way to meet some of the other teachers you'll be working with. "Why do you arrange your desks this way?" might not be the most exciting conversation starter, but you'll quickly find that it's something every teacher has an opinion on!

While the way you arrange your desks in large part depends on your room's size and shape and the number of students you have, figure 1.1 offers four common seating arrangements to consider, and a few pros and cons on each.

Good Ol' Rows	Rows In Pairs (or Shoulder Partners)
Front of classroom	*Front of classroom*
Benefits	**Benefits**
• It's easy to walk through rows and see students.	• It's easy to walk through rows and see students.
• You can see all students at all times.	• You can see all students at all times.
• Students from first grade on are probably familiar with this setup.	• Students have a shoulder partner to learn from and support.
Drawbacks	**Drawbacks**
• Student interaction is limited.	• Student interaction is limited.
• This makes it challenging to do group work; students have to move desks.	• Students often end up working with the same person, though this could also be a benefit.
• Taller students usually need to be placed toward the back of the room.	• When a shoulder partner is absent, you might need to move present students to fill in a seat.

Figure 1.1: Common seating arrangements.

Continued ▶

Tables of Four	Horseshoe
Front of classroom 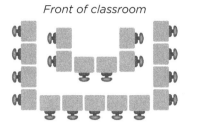	*Front of classroom*
Benefits • Gives the classroom a team feel. • You can see all students at all times. • This encourages interaction and learning from each other. **Drawbacks** • Students can get distracted by each other. • Students might have to turn their heads to see the front of the classroom. • Determining which student to put in which group can be a challenge.	**Benefits** • Students can see each other and it encourages students to speak to the entire class. • You can see all students at all times. • It's easy to distribute and collect materials, since everyone can just pass to the left or collect from the right. **Drawbacks** • Students who do not feel comfortable speaking in front of entire class may be extra hesitant. • Square, oddly shaped, or smaller classrooms make it challenging to arrange desks this way. • It's tough to move around the entire classroom, since you have to walk through the whole horseshoe.

Of course, your classroom—especially in kindergarten and the lower grades—might include a reading nook, cool-down station, or another setup that students can use outside of their normal seating arrangement. Wherever you place this station, make sure it doesn't obstruct anyone's view or ability to move around the room safely.

And remember, there's always a new student on the way! Students new to your classroom often transfer in midyear, so either have an extra desk or two ready to incorporate into your seating arrangement, or keep a seat open and ready. Of course, you'll also have students transfer out of your classroom midyear as well, so hopefully things won't be too crowded when that new student arrives.

Use a Seating Chart

New teachers especially often wonder if they should use a seating chart, as some educators feel that allowing students to select their own seats can be empowering. Some experienced teachers might joke that allowing students to choose their own seats immediately shows the teacher who they should *not* allow to sit together. Regardless, when it comes to deciding whether to use a seating chart, our answer is an emphatic *yes*.

Using a seating chart has three clear advantages.

1. It helps you immediately know who is present and who to mark absent.

2. It helps you learn everyone's name quickly, and you can easily refer to it if you forget a student's name.

3. When there is a substitute teacher in your class, that person can easily take attendance and keep track of students.

Using a seating chart also sets the tone that you are well organized and sends a clear message to the students that you are in charge of the classroom. Students will know you are determined to know who is where at all times. And just because you start the year or semester with a seating chart doesn't mean that chart can't change. Your seating chart is a living, breathing, ever-changing document, so either write the students' names in pencil, erasable ink, or in a digital format that can be easily changed.

You'll be constantly switching students' seats once you see how your seating chart plays out in real time. Some students are too tall to sit in the front; other students need to move so they can better see or hear, and of course, some combinations of students are just too chatty to sit near each other.

When you move a student (or a few students), do it with poise and confidence, and be mindful not to call out specific characteristics. You can simply say, "I want to try something new. Marcus, I'm going to have you switch seats with Isabella." Consider making the change quietly at the beginning of class—it only needs to involve Marcus and Isabella—so it doesn't disrupt the rest of the class. Of course, there might be times when you need to switch in the middle of class, and that's OK. Again, project confidence and clarity when you have students switch, and they'll usually follow your lead.

Tips to Thrive

At the beginning of the school year (or whenever you begin teaching the class), consider arranging students on your seating chart alphabetically by *first* name. This might help you learn all the students' first names quickly, and their last names naturally follow. If a student in the first row asks a question and you're not near your seating chart, you know it's going to be a name toward the front of the alphabet, like Alonzo or Chris. Student in the back row? That's probably William or Yessenia!

Think About What to Put On the Walls

The wall spaces in your classroom aren't just there to separate you from other class-rooms. They are a canvas that can invite students into the joy of learning. In the TV show *Abbott Elementary*, teacher Janine Teagues says, "The walls are the soul of the classroom" (Murphy & Einhorn, 2022).

Consider the opportunities your classroom walls offer—opportunities for you to communicate with all who enter what is most important, what you are teaching, and how things will run. Research reveals the "importance of a classroom's symbolic features, such as objects and wall décor, in influencing student learning and achievement in that environment" (Cheryan, Ziegler, Plaut, & Meltzoff, 2014).

Keep the following three items in mind when deciding what to put up on your walls: (1) keep it simple, (2) devote prime wall space to what is most important, and (3) point things out.

Keep It Simple

Just because you have the wall space doesn't mean you have to fill it. Putting up too much can often be distracting and frustrating for students. Research indicates that students in a environment not saturated with visuals are better able to focus (Rodrigues & Pandeirada, 2018).

Be as intentional as possible about everything you put up. Ask yourself the following questions.

- "Will this help my students learn? Is it a learning strategy or something that students are currently learning about?"
- "Will this make my classroom more inviting and interesting?"
- "Will this add to the overall vibe (culture, message, or so on) I'm going for?"

If you don't answer *yes* to at least one of the questions, leave it off the wall until you find something that applies.

Devote Prime Wall Space to What Is Most Important

What are the most important things that you want students to see every day? Put them toward the front of the classroom, where students spend the most time looking. Have a chart or something that you'll refer to on occasion? Consider putting that on a side wall, so students can easily see it but don't need to see it all the time. Photos of you, your pet, and your family? Leave those behind your desk. It's not that photos of you, your pet, and family aren't important, it's just that learning about them isn't the primary reason students come to school each day, so they shouldn't get the prime space on your walls.

Here are some of the most important items to display every day.

- **Classroom expectations:** Properly managing your classroom (more on that in chapter 3, page 31) means increasing the chances of things running smoothly. Everyone showing respect helps ensure that. Posted expectations for student behavior serve as a good, visual reminder to students about their choices, and you can easily refer to the expectations when they're posted in front of everyone.
- **Agenda:** Displaying the agenda for the class or day saves you time and work, especially when you train students to look at what you've posted each day as they enter the classroom. They'll clearly see what you have planned, and you'll never (or less commonly) have to answer the question, "What are we doing today?"

- **Learning goals, targets, or objectives:** As obvious as it sounds, students need to know what they're learning. Put it right in front of them! This also makes it easy to refer to the goal throughout the class and help keep *you* on track as well.

- **Classwork and homework:** The clearer and more obvious you can make assignments, the more likely students will be to complete them on time. Posting them in the same place each day also makes it easier for students to keep track of everything, as they'll know to always look in the same place.

- **Important reminders (like due dates):** Posting these helps keep everyone on schedule, and putting them where they are visible to everyone conveys their importance.

- **The date:** How else would anyone know what day it is?

Predictability is part of feeling safe (Orchard & Souers, 2020). Students should never have to wonder where you'll post the day's objectives, agenda, or assignment. Find a good spot where everyone can see them and update them as often as needed. This also means putting them in a spot where you can easily change them each day.

Point Things Out

Sure, you took all that time to hang it on the wall, but don't assume that means the students will automatically see it. It's up to you to point it out and continue referring to it as often as needed. When you hang up some student work, be sure to say, "Make sure to check out the work samples I hung up on the back wall from some of your classmates" (and physically point to the samples while you're talking). When you mention, "Today's learning goal is . . . ," stand right next to it and point to it, so students know exactly where to find it (and where they can always find it in the future). Of course, you should adjust the words based on your students' ages.

And when a student isn't fulfilling one of the classroom expectations, it can be much more effective to simply point to the expectations (and have a stern look on your face) as a good reminder of its importance, emphasizing nonverbally that's it's been posted there all along. And it saves you from having to constantly raise your voice, or even talk at all.

Plan for Where to Place Classroom Materials and Supplies

You've probably heard that teachers often spend their own money on classroom supplies. In one informal poll, veteran teachers report wishing "they spent less of their own money on their classrooms" (Moore, 2021). So, while this definitely happens, you do *not* want to spend money on anything that isn't absolutely essential. The good news is that you don't need to have a perfectly decorated classroom. Your book bins don't have to be multiple colors or all match, for example. And, if you are going to spend your own money, make sure it's something that will truly add value to your classroom.

Here are ideas for ways to save money on supplies.

- Let your friends and neighbors know that you're a teacher now, and that you would like to know if they're thinking about getting rid of a piece of furniture. The piece might just be something you can use in your classroom.

- Use websites like Donors Choose (www.donorschoose.org), which allows you to post your class projects and needs and be matched with those who want to help fund them.

- Introduce yourself to the manager at your local office supplies store. Let them know you're a teacher and see if they are willing to donate supplies. If they do, follow it up with a thank-you note from yourself and your students. You might just get more donations in the years that follow.

What you need for your classroom depends in a big way on the age of your students, the subjects you're teaching, and the activities you're planning. The following sections offer guidance for locating the good stuff.

- Start with what's there.

- Find the supply closet.

- Locate your books and curricula.

- Determine your technology needs.

- Find inspiration and other things that keep you going.

- Organize your own desk and personal space.

Start With What's There

In many cases, you'll find things in your classroom from the previous year or teacher—everything from bookshelves to notebooks. You might even find a few candy bars stuffed in the back drawer of the teacher's desk (but we *don't* recommend eating them). Look around your classroom and take a good inventory of what's already there. This frees you up to focus on what you still need.

It's OK if you don't feel like you have everything that you need. As the school year progresses, you'll continue building your inventory and get good at figuring out where to get items and who to ask for what you need. Remember that getting all the supplies and materials you and your students need is an ongoing process, and you might even find yourself getting rid of things you don't need to make space for the things you do! Getting rid of things can be quite easy: email colleagues a photo of the item or post a photo of it in the staff lounge and see if anyone wants your items. You could also reach out to your school's custodian to see if they can remove a larger item.

Find the Supply Closet

You'll need things like pens, paper, staplers, and scissors—you get the idea. Many schools have a supply room where you can get what you need. Some might require you to fill out a request form before and the supplies are then delivered to your room. Find out where this room is, and just as important, find out who holds the key to this room. In many cases, it will be the school secretary or custodian. Don't be shy about asking for what you need. Your success depends on it!

Locate Your Books and Curricula

Even in a world with endless websites, videos, and apps, most schools have a central curriculum from which teachers base their lessons. This curriculum, often determined by the district, state, or province you teach in, can serve as a good guide in determining what you teach and the order in which you teach it. Of course, *how* you teach it is the most exciting part, and we cover that in chapter 5 (page 57).

Books and curricula are often distributed through the school's library. In some schools, the librarian or office staff might have an organized distribution method; in other schools, you might need to ask another teacher what to do. Once you know what subjects and levels you'll be teaching, make sure you have enough books for all of your students— and be sure to have some extras on hand for students who transfer into your classroom midyear.

As your teaching career progresses, especially if you're teaching early elementary, you'll start building a classroom library with books for both your students and yourself. This takes time, but by constantly adding to your library, it won't be long before you have an impressive shelf (or several shelves) filled with books. Of course, with the rise of online and hybrid learning, some schools and classes have moved completely to digital texts. While this is certainly easier on the back (no lugging around several textbooks), there might be times when you want students to read or look over a hard copy. You can always print and hand out the section that students need.

Determine Your Technology Needs

Many schools and districts provide the technology (or at least some of it) that you'll need as a teacher. Many schools distribute laptops to each teacher, and classrooms often come equipped with desktop computers or a digital whiteboard. Perhaps, eventually, you'll have a robot or droid as a teaching assistant. Often, the district employs a technology coordinator, or someone with a similar title, who can help you get what you need and get things fixed when something breaks. Find out who this person is and put them on your list of the most important staff members to know on campus, along with your school's custodian.

Although using two computers might be a bit confusing at first, separating your work device from your personal device is a good idea. It prevents those photos that you took at your cousin's wedding from popping up during one of your class lessons, and on nights that you leave your work laptop at school, you'll still have access to your home computer, but might not feel the need to be constantly working.

Tips to Thrive

Technology can be a wonderful teaching tool that opens up incredible learning opportunities for you and your students and helps you stay organized. It can also be frustrating. Devices break, internet connections can be unreliable, and countless things can distract us. Learn to manage these frustrations and try to have a backup plan for when things go awry.

Internet not working, so you can't show a video? Be ready with a story that you can read to students.

Online game not working properly? Be prepared with a tabletop or other kind of game you and your students can play.

And if all else fails, always have paper and some pencils ready.

Find Inspiration and Other Things That Keep You Going

Perhaps there's a famous quote that you love, an inspiring photo, or a mantra that speaks to you. Consider hanging it on the wall to keep you going. The back of the classroom is a nice place to put such items. You'll have a clear view of it from the front of the classroom (or wherever you are), and your students will see it as they enter or exit. Just make sure it's big enough to see. It can also be a powerful reminder for the students. Even though you might have heard the quote or seen the image many times, for many of your students, it might be the very first time.

Organize Your Own Desk and Personal Space

Your desk is the command center of the classroom. Although you won't spend the majority of your time at it while you're teaching, it is where you begin and end most days, conduct student and parent conferences, and retreat sometimes when you just need a moment to take a deep breath and recenter yourself.

Here are a few tips to set up your own space for success.

- **Arrange your desk off to the side of the classroom or in the back:** Just don't put it front and center. Leave that space open for all the teaching you'll be doing when students are present.

- **Position your desk and chair so you can see all your students while sitting:** This is critically important during times when you might be meeting with a student at your desk. You'll be able to keep track of everything that is happening in your classroom with a single glance. (Read more about that in chapter 2, page 17, and chapter 4, page 45).

- **Be sure you can see your classroom door (or doors) from your desk:** Most of the time that you're at your desk is when students are not in the classroom, so you want to make sure you are able to see and greet anyone who enters. Nobody should ever be able to sneak up on you!

- **Make sure you can get to and from your desk area quickly and safely:** You may have to grab something from or take care of something at your desk. Be sure that all pathways are clear.

- **Have a safe place for your valuable stuff:** That may be a drawer in your desk or filing cabinet that locks or is at least a bit tucked away. Use it to store your personal items, and try to avoid using the space while students are in the classroom. Even the most beloved (and feared) teachers on campus have had things stolen over the years. You might even consider investing in a small safe to install somewhere in your classroom, if there isn't a lockable space in your desk or cabinet.

- **It's OK to have boundaries:** Your space is yours, and it's fine to ask students not to sit in your chair or go behind your desk. Just make sure you are firm and clear when communicating this to students—and enforce it consistently. Don't let one student go behind your desk to grab something, but not let another.

Like the rest of your classroom, make your desk a place where you feel comfortable and enjoy sitting that allows you to work efficiently and find what you need.

Final Thoughts: Ideas Are Everywhere

Remember that how you set up your classroom is a consistently evolving and improving process. Don't be afraid to try something new and change things around (and sometimes, change them back to how they were)!

Always be on the lookout for new ideas. Anytime you walk into a colleague's classroom, go into immediate analysis mode. Check out how they've arranged their walls, desks, and everything else. If you can, ask that teacher about it, and even take a quick photo for reference.

When you see something you like that could work for you, take the idea and make it your own. Over time, your classroom will become a place that students love walking into, enjoy being a part of, and remember for years to come. And above all, always make sure that your classroom is safe and clean and that everyone can be seen.

CHAPTER 2

How Can I Build Relationships With Students?

Building relationships with students is the key to successful teaching. It's also what makes this work most fulfilling and memorable. Each year, your classroom will be filled with students who make you laugh, cry, and give you a deepened insight into the world that we live in. While there are a lot of definitions of what a *relationship* is, one word that stands out most is *connection*.

From the moment you first meet your students (and sometimes even before that), a connection is made. From that moment on, you have an opportunity to build on and strengthen that connection with your students. Of course, that means that the connection can also weaken. While there are many small and large facets that go into connecting with students, here are three foundational pillars that form the basis of strong relationships.

- **Valuing time together:** Strong relationships are built over time through countless interactions and reactions made in real time. Whether in person or virtual, each day is an opportunity to spend some time with students.

- **Being interested and interesting:** Every student has a story, and if you make it your mission to discover that story, you will find each is wonderfully interesting, filled with ideas and creative thoughts that can empower you to support their learning. At the same time, we, as teachers, are amazingly interesting as well. We all have our own experiences and stories we can use to keep students engaged and on the edge of their seats! Building strong relationships with students requires us to see the "interesting" in our students and find ways to make sure they see it in us as well.

- **Building trust:** Acclaimed author and leadership expert Rachel Botsman (2017) defines *trust* as "a confident relationship with the unknown" (p. 20). Building strong relationships with our students requires them to trust us and for us to trust them. Each day is an opportunity to build upon and strengthen this trust.

Keep in mind the words of professor James Comer (1995), who famously said, "No significant learning can occur without a significant relationship." With that, the following tips in this chapter help you develop all three of these relationship pillars, building strong and powerful relationships with your students.

- Pronounce students' names correctly.
- Know students' DNA.
- Use what you know to build connections and further learning.
- Say "Hello."
- Say "Goodbye."
- Know a bit about students' living situation.
- Tell stories.
- Show your stuff.
- Just ask.
- Be real.
- Remember the hidden relationships that exist in the classroom.

Don't feel like you need to do all of these every day. Start with those you are most comfortable with and build on them as the weeks progress.

Pronounce Students' Names Correctly

Some students have names that are easy to pronounce. Other students have names that are difficult to pronounce. Making the effort to pronounce all of our students' names correctly has a tremendous impact on the relationships we build with them. Moreover, constant mispronunciation not only makes school more stressful, it can send a message that teachers aren't respecting students' identity, culture, and heritage (McFarlane, 2023).

It can be very empowering for a student when a teacher takes the time to learn to say their name correctly, and even if you don't get it right every time, the students will respect and appreciate your effort. At the same time, it can be degrading for a student when a teacher decides that they won't be able to pronounce a student's name and instead comes up with a shortened version or a nickname. A student's social-emotional well-being is harmed when a teacher says their name incorrectly (Hodge, 2020).

Derald Wing Sue and colleagues (2007) speak of the significant concern that can arise (even unintentionally) when they suggest that name mispronunciation falls into the larger category of *microaggressions*, which they define as "brief and commonplace daily verbal, behavioral, or environmental indignities, whether intentional or unintentional, that communicate hostile, derogatory, or negative racial slights and insults toward people of color" (p. 271). The intent may be so far off your radar as to be unthinkable; however, the impact can be with a student forever. When we take the time to learn to pronounce a student's name correctly, we are taking the time to get to know them, to truly begin to see them, and this is incredibly important (take it from the book's authors, whose last names are Kajitani and Hierck).

Here are a few suggestions on how to make sure you pronounce your students' names correctly.

- **Look over your class rosters in advance:** When you see a name that might be hard to pronounce, see if you can work out how to say it aloud. Other teachers who previously had that student in their class can be a big help as well.

- **Ask students to pronounce their names:** Tell the students that it's very important to you that you pronounce their names correctly, and ask them to pronounce their names for you. Write out their names phonetically on a roster that only you see. If you don't want to single out students, have all of them write down their names, as well as how to pronounce it phonetically on a note card. Or better yet, tie it in with a language arts lesson on phonetics.

- **Say something positive:** When you ask a student who has what you consider a hard-to-pronounce name what their name is, immediately follow it up with something positive, such as "What a great name!" or "Wow! How did your name come to be?" This helps you be interested and be interesting.

Know Students' DNA

It's critical to know the importance of learning every student's *DNA*—their dreams, needs, and abilities: "To discover student strengths, teachers need to talk to their students and learn what skills, talents, character traits, and assets they bring to the classroom" (Eller & Hierck, 2021, p. 43). This allows you to structure your lessons around these strengths and interests.

You have infinite effective ways to do this, but one we suggest is to provide students with a simple template that has the three letters, DNA, written on it. After explaining what these letters stand for, invite students to list items corresponding to each letter. Encourage them to be authentic and not supply the answers they think adults might want to hear (for example, all students say their dream is to become a doctor); instead, have them honestly share their thoughts and wishes.

The exercise in figure 2.1 (page 20) provides you with great insight into each student, which you can use in building lessons throughout their year of learning. (See the next section.) You and your teacher colleagues might even share this information with each other or even post display boards outside each classroom listing fun facts about your students. If the DNA sheet in figure 2.1 were outside your classroom door, would it help colleagues get to know *all* students and not just *their* students?

Dreams

I want to learn everything I can about video game design and coding.

Needs

I need help learning to read better and staying organized.

Abilities

I can draw well, and people tell me I am funny.

Figure 2.1: DNA worksheet.

*Visit **go.SolutionTree.com/teacherefficacy** for a free reproducible version of this figure.*

Regardless of your approach, be mindful and respectful of students' privacy. This can be a positive, affirming activity, but always check with students first before sharing or posting any information about your students. Sensitive or otherwise personal information should always be kept private, but also be mindful that, as teachers, we don't always know what information students might feel sensitive about sharing. Respect this.

In the simplest terms, an asset-based approach focuses on strengths we identify in all our students—and they *all* have strengths. Diversity in thought, culture, and traits are positive assets from which all students and adults can benefit. Members of the classroom community should be valued for what they bring to the classroom rather than defined by negative attributes. School can be a stressful time for students. Sometimes they speak entirely different languages at home than they do in school, or maybe they have abilities that might be a departure from the perceived norm. Students from trauma situations may interpret seemingly commonplace adult behaviors as aggression and react accordingly. And any elements outside of students' perceived norm can result in them feeling peer pressure to behave and act in certain ways. For example, a student may have just experienced a traumatic event right before school but will need to put on a happy face so peers and teachers don't see the pain.

And while school can be stressful, confusing, and complicated for some students, keep in mind that it is also the place where they can be welcomed and seen and can work through many of the challenges they are experiencing. When we help students identify their DNA and support their work toward their goals, we build powerful relationships with them.

Use What You Know to Build Connections and Further Learning

It might seem pretty obvious that gathering your students' DNA so that you begin to understand what they are interested in is an important component of building strong relationships with them. The truly powerful step is taking that knowledge and bringing it up from time to time. You don't need to have long, in-depth conversations with students. A simple "Hey Maria, how did your soccer tournament go this past weekend?" sends a clear message to Maria that her teacher sees her and is interested in her life.

Of course, the real magic happens when you can somehow link your students' interests to the academic content that you're teaching. If you're teaching a lesson on fractions, and you also know that your student Julio loves to cook, take a moment at the beginning of the lesson and say, "I know a lot of you, like Julio, love to cook. Today we're going to be learning about fractions, which are a huge part of cooking." (Bonus points for holding up some different measuring cups!)

The next time Julio and the rest of your students are cooking and grab a measuring cup, they'll think of you and apply that amazing lesson about fractions.

Say "Hello"

As obvious as saying "Hello" might sound, it is also one of the most powerful strategies for building relationships. Have you ever walked into a restaurant and nobody was there to greet you? You probably stood there awkwardly until someone finally came. Even if you have to wait a minute, it feels like an hour. What a relief when someone finally does arrive and greets you. (Be sure to see the Tips to Thrive, page 34, for more on greeting students at the door.)

Greeting a student, especially as they're walking into your classroom, sends a clear message that you see this person, value them, and are happy they're at school. Of course, students will pick up on the tone and manner in which you greet them, and even though it's only one word, saying it with positivity and enthusiasm can make a big difference in a student's day.

Of course, there are many different ways to say "Hello," so don't limit yourself to just that word. However you decide to greet someone, your students will see the effort you are making, and hopefully greet you back. (And even if they don't, they'll know that you see them.)

Tips to Thrive

Sometimes, you might not be excited to see a certain student (or a few of them). Maybe something didn't go well the day before, and you're still a bit angry about it. Remember that every day is a chance to press the reset button with even your more challenging students. Keep in mind that the same student is aware that things didn't go well yesterday and is likely very nervous to see you. Even if you feel angry or resentful of the student (it happens!) offering a simple and friendly "Hello [name]," tells that student that you're still their teacher, you're still looking out for them, and they're still welcome in your classroom.

Say "Goodbye"

Have you ever left a party or social gathering without saying goodbye to the host, or other people there? It can feel awkward and even rude. As teachers, we often run out of time at the end of the day or at the end of a class and aren't able to offer some form of farewell to all of our students. But saying goodbye gives closure, and when it's attached to "see you tomorrow," it sends a clear message and expectation that you'll be as excited for the next time you see your students as you were when they arrived that day.

Of course, saying goodbye to every student at the end of the day or class might be logistically difficult, so consider having a fun end-of-class mantra or chant that you all do, to bring closure to the day. It can be as simple as saying, "OK, everyone wave and say 'goodbye' on the count of three: one . . . two . . . three!" Everyone then shouts "Goodbye!" together.

Remember, for students who have challenging living situations, a goodbye from you might be the last time an adult acknowledges them until they return to school the next day. Never underestimate how powerful a simple and warm greeting or send-off can be for our students—and for ourselves.

Know a Bit About Students' Living Situation

A few years ago, Alex had a student in class named Luis (whose name, as well as other students', has been changed). On the very last day of the school year, Alex's school held a morning graduation ceremony for the eighth graders and their families, then told the students they could go home early and start their summer. With the students now gone, Alex had a few extra hours to begin packing up the classroom. A few minutes after returning to the classroom, Luis popped his head in and asked if he could hang out until lunchtime. Alex assured him he could but asked him why he would want to do that when he could start his summer instead.

Luis looked down and said, "I just want to eat the free lunch one more time before I go home all summer to nothing." It was at that moment that Alex realized that Luis was in the class period right before lunch; having just learned Luis's family had food insecurity, he understood that Luis must have been sitting there, very hungry, each day. As his teacher, Alex was not empowered to impact Luis's life at home, but had Alex known this situation, he could have quietly slipped him a granola bar to help get him through until lunch.

As you've seen from previous sections in this chapter, very often, it's the smallest gestures that can keep a student going as they work through adversity. There are so many reasons for the mindsets our students come to school with, and knowing a bit about their living situations can help us understand on a deeper level what they're going through. It's hard to get mad at a student who didn't complete their homework when you know they are the main care provider for their two younger siblings. Such knowledge inevitably changes the conversation you have with that student, opening up creative ways to help them get that work done.

In a different example, it also shifts the way you respond to a student who acts out in class when you know their mom is going through cancer treatments. You don't have to know everything about everyone, and you can't force students to trust you with information that is sensitive and personal to them, but there are probing questions you can ask. Here are five such questions that will enable you to find out more about a student's living situation and the information the question intends to uncover.

- **"Who do you live with?"** This question addresses the family dynamic that the student is living with. If a student says they live with their mom, it allows you to follow up by asking how often they see their dad.

- **"What do you like to do on weekends?"** This question is a great way to find out more about students' interests that you might not get from the DNA worksheet.

- **"What are your favorite holidays to celebrate?"** This question can provide insight into a student's ethnicity and culture.

- **"Do you speak any languages other than English at home?"** This question provides information about whether a student is an English learner and where they may have lived previously.

- **"Do you live somewhere that can receive mail?"** This is a softer way to ask a student if they are currently unhoused or if they're moving around from house to house.

Note that these questions are best asked privately, not in front of the entire class. For that reason, you may prefer to give students a quick question worksheet to fill out (with questions like those in the Question column in figure 2.2). In the right column here you can see what the answer may uncover. Visit **go.SolutionTree.com/teacherefficacy** for a free reproducible, titled "About Me", that leaves the right column blank for students to write in.

Question	What the Answer Uncovers
Who do you live with?	The family dynamic that the student is living with. If a student says they live with their mom, it allows you to follow up with asking how often they see their dad.
What do you like to do on weekends?	A great way to find out about students' interests.
What are your favorite holidays to celebrate?	Can provide good insight into a student's ethnicity and culture.
Do you speak any languages other than English at home?	Provides good insight into whether they are an English learner and where they may have lived prior to now.
Do you live somewhere that can receive mail?	A much softer way to ask a student if they are currently unhoused or moving around from house to house.

Figure 2.2: Learning about a student's living situation.

*Visit **go.SolutionTree.com/teacherefficacy** for a free reproducible version of this figure.*

Tell a Story

Everyone loves a good story. Stories help us connect, visualize, and make sense of the world. They're also fun to tell and hard to forget! When used strategically and appropriately, a good story can bring the academic content that you are teaching to life while helping to build strong relationships with your students. It doesn't need to be an epic tale of the time you did something incredible—it can be a seemingly small story that reinforces what you're teaching in class or something you feel is important for the students to know about you (remember, keep it to class-appropriate stories only).

In addition, the stories you tell don't need to be about you. They can be about someone else, or you can retell a story that you heard on the news, or it can be something you read. You also don't need to tell every story with perfect delivery—but you will notice that the more times you tell a story, the better you'll get at it! Consider the following examples.

- **Teaching a lesson about decimals?** Tell the story about that time you (or someone you knew) accidentally put the decimal in the wrong place and paid $160.00 instead of $16.00.

- **Teaching a lesson about punctuation and comma placement?** Tell the students about the time you accidentally texted "Let's eat Grandma" instead of "Let's eat, Grandma!" (OK, that's an old joke, but it makes the point pretty well, and your students are sure to remember it.)

- **Teaching about geography?** Perhaps you have a photo of yourself in a location that you're teaching about. Show students the photo, and tell them a story about something that happened while you were there. Again, it doesn't need to be a story about you; it can be about something that happened to your friend, family member, or anyone else.

You get the idea. Just keep in mind that after you tell a story, the students might offer a few stories of their own.

Show Your Stuff

Just as a good story brings our imaginations to life, and helps to reinforce the details of what we're learning, bringing in real "stuff" that you have a connection to and that students can see and touch is another great way to help build relationships with students. Often referred to as *realia*, or real-life objects that enable students to make connections to their own lives, it's also a great strategy to help students understand the content that you're teaching because you're bringing in authentic objects that bring content to life.

The stuff you show doesn't need to be anything fancy or amazing. Is there a pizza place in town that you love? Grab a few takeout menus and bring them in, and show them to your students the next time you're talking about diameter. ("Do you want the 12" or the 14" pizza?") Your students will not only think of you the next time they order a pizza (especially if it's from that place or they drive by it), but they might also think just a little differently about how the diameter equates to how much food they have. Now you're building the relationship *and* reinforcing the concepts that students are learning.

Just Ask

Used effectively, questions are powerful tools. There will be days when a normally enthusiastic student looks a bit down. Take a moment and ask them how they're doing today. Maybe something is going on, and they tell you. Maybe something is going on, and they don't tell you. Or maybe there's nothing going on, and you just caught them in a tired moment. Regardless, the fact that you asked shows that student that you are paying attention and looking out for them.

The tool in figure 2.3 shows an example of a 2 × 4 relationship-building activity; it is a great way to connect with your students and to track that you have connected with all of them at regular intervals. This activity suggests that a teacher will connect with four students each day for two minutes. Here's the key—the connection or focal point of the conversation has nothing to do with what's going on in the lesson and is all about talking about what interests the student. This helps connect and strengthen relationships with your students.

Be Real

It may take a bit of time, but students eventually know when their teachers are faking it. Even when everything seems to happen at a pace that's hard to keep up with and disinformation is everywhere, our students can tell the difference between those who are looking to authentically connect and those who aren't. There are a lot of references to teachers being superheroes and life changers. While there are moments where we feel like both (and often, we are), we also have plenty of days where we struggle, make mistakes, and get frustrated. It's OK, and you're not alone.

Being real doesn't mean you have to disclose everything that is happening in your life to your students (that is definitely not recommended). But allowing yourself to be (appropriately) honest with students and, on occasion, to be vulnerable in front of them can lead to the kind of trust that is essential to building strong relationships.

In her research, author and social-emotional learning researcher Brené Brown (2015) finds that trust and vulnerability are inextricably linked. For trust to exist in a relationship, individuals must allow themselves to be vulnerable with those same people (Brown, 2015). Of course, your students are not your adult friends, there is often a significant age difference between you and your students, and you've been hired to do a job. So, here are a few ways that you can be real without inappropriately oversharing with your students.

- **Do what you say you will do:** Not much more to say on this one. When we do what we say we will do, we build trust. When we don't, we lose trust. It's a simple equation.

- **When you make a mistake, own it and move forward:** From making calculation errors while teaching mathematics to forgetting that stack of graded essays at home (that you *promised* you would have back to your students by today) to making a bad judgment call about how to handle a situation that arises in class, teachers make mistakes all the time. When you do, own it. Say, "Well, I messed that one up—sorry about that." Follow that up with, "Let's move forward, and I'll get it right next time." Don't spend too much time dwelling on it. Your students will appreciate your honesty, and they'll learn to do the same when they make a mistake.

Teacher:
Grade or course:

Directions: Aim to spend two minutes a day with four different students talking to them as individuals about their lives. You can use the questions as a way to generate discussion. Use this chart to list the names of students to meet with each day and use these conversations to get to know each student and to let them better get to know you. Focus conversation around out-of-school activities. At the end of the calendar, reflect on what you learned about each student and how you can use that information to provide additional support in the classroom. Of course, there are many more questions you can (and should) ask, but these will get you started connecting with your students.

Questions you can ask:
- What's your favorite way to spend an hour?
- If you could only eat one meal for the rest of your life, what would it be?
- Who, or what, is inspiring you these days?
- What's the biggest challenge you've overcome in your life?
- What's one of the best books you've ever read or movies or shows you've ever watched?

Monthly Schedule

Monday	Tuesday	Wednesday	Thursday	Friday
Monday	**Tuesday**	**Wednesday**	**Thursday**	**Friday**
Monday	**Tuesday**	**Wednesday**	**Thursday**	**Friday**
Monday	**Tuesday**	**Wednesday**	**Thursday**	**Friday**

Source: © 2019 by Greg Wolcott. Adapted with permission.

Figure 2.3: The 2 × 4 relationship-building activity.

*Visit **go.SolutionTree.com/teacherefficacy** for a free reproducible version of this figure.*

- **Say "Please" and "Thank you":** Everyone likes to be respected and appreciated. That goes for a kindergartener who you are asking to clean up their desk, to a high school student who you are, uh, asking to clean up their desk. Whenever we ask someone to do something, including a genuine "please" and closing with a heartfelt "thank you" can make all the difference in how that person responds and how the relationship is built. Most importantly, your students will learn to do the same.

Remember the Hidden Relationships That Exist in the Classroom

While the majority of this chapter is devoted to how teachers can build relationships with their students, keep in mind that there are a few other relationships that are happening in a classroom at any given moment that you may not always see: students' relationships with content (ours as well) and students' relationships with each other (ours as well).

Build Students' Relationship With the Content

Not every one of your students will walk into your class loving the lessons you have planned or the subject you teach. They might even tell you they hate it. Don't stress about this—they haven't had *you* as their teacher yet! Just as each day is an opportunity to build relationships with students, each day is also an opportunity to build a student's relationship with the content (and some days will go better than others). Be sure to check out chapter 5 (page 57) on creating engaging lessons for your students.

As a teacher, you'll have your own relationship with the content. The first few times you teach something, you'll probably feel a bit shaky with the information, and that's OK and totally normal. You'll continue to get more comfortable with it each day. Over the years, there will also be specific topics that you love teaching, and others that you're not crazy about. Again, that's OK and totally normal.

Help Students Build Relationships With Each Other

Ever had a job, or a class, where you really enjoyed working with your coworkers? It can turn a normally mundane job into something that you actually look forward to. At the same time, it's pretty tough for a student to focus on learning about irony and alliterations when they've just gotten into an argument with their friend or if they're uncomfortable with the person they're sitting next to. Remember that your students' relationships exist and develop outside your classroom, and those experiences can have an impact on what happens inside your classroom. Often, those are positive experiences, and often they're not.

While it might not be what you list in the daily objectives or put on a test, creating opportunities for students to build relationships or mend fences with each other can have a significant impact on how they feel about being in your class. Giving them a chance to talk to each other (be sure to see chapter 5, on creating engaging lessons for some ideas on how to do this), share their experiences, and learn from each other can help build a classroom culture where students feel safe, feel confident, and look forward to each day.

Final Thoughts: The Moments That Matter

From time to time, a student will come back to visit you after being in your class a few or several years prior. They'll be taller, older, and more capable (hopefully). They probably won't remember the lessons, the homework, or the grade they got in your class. But they will remember certain moments. Moments they laughed, moments they cried, moments that are ingrained in their memories because of something you said or how you treated them. What they are remembering is the relationship you built with them.

Each day is an opportunity to build and strengthen relationships with your students. From the simple acts of saying "Hello" and "Goodbye" to taking the time to incorporate their interests into the lesson you're teaching, the connections you make with your students will help you be highly effective as a teacher and nourish your soul as a person.

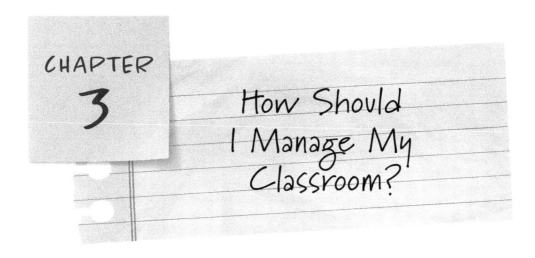

CHAPTER

3

How Should
I Manage My
Classroom?

In the preceding chapter, we focused on the importance of prioritizing and developing one-on-one relationships with your students to build trust and a stronger foundation for learning. But those individual relationships are only one part of the big picture when it comes to how you relate to students. As a teacher, your ability to manage your classroom as a whole will be one of the biggest factors in your success and the success of your students. Luckily, "there is evidence that teachers' skills are more predictive for their management actions in the classroom than their knowledge" (Stahnke & Blömeke, 2021).

Have you ever driven by a store with a big sign across the front that says *Under New Management*? Think about the message that sign conveys—the store and everything inside it is essentially the same, but the store is run differently now. The people leading it are somehow different, and despite any negative experiences you (as a customer) might have had in the past, you should come back and try it again. When you think about it, this dynamic isn't wholly different for the students entering your classroom at the start of a new year or new semester. You can manage your classroom in lots of ways. Some teachers manage their classroom in a strict, top-down approach where they insist that students follow every direction at every moment. Some teachers give their students more room to make their own decisions and don't mind a bit of extra noise and chatter to allow that to happen. And some teachers, well—let's just say *the students run the classroom* while the teacher is just hanging on, trying to get through each lesson, until the final bell rings!

Respected educators Harry and Rosemary Wong (2018) define *classroom management* as the "practices and procedures that a teacher uses to maintain an environment in which instruction and learning can occur" (p. 8). This is different from *behavior management*, which professor of leadership and teacher education R. Allan Allday describes as the "techniques used by educators to promote appropriate behaviors and discourage inappropriate behaviors" (R. A. Allday, personal communication with Chelonnda Seroyer, October 27, 2015). Behavior management is addressed in chapter 4 (page 45). In short, classroom management is how you run your classroom, and behavior management is how you prepare for and respond when students don't behave according to your expectations.

While both classroom management and behavior management are inextricably linked, this chapter focuses primarily on classroom management, with an emphasis on the following ideas.

- Accept that imposter syndrome is totally normal.
- Determine necessary classroom procedures and routines.
- Teach classroom procedures and routines to students.
- Project confidence.

We discuss aspects and strategies for behavior management in chapter 4.

Accept That Imposter Syndrome Is Totally Normal

As a new teacher, there will be moments, class periods, and perhaps even entire days where you feel like you have absolutely no idea what you're doing. As we've said a few times (and will say a few more times), it's OK, and it's totally normal. *Imposter syndrome* occurs when someone believes they are inadequate and incompetent "despite evidence that indicates [they are] skilled and quite successful" (Wilding, 2022).

Every day, you're expected to help students learn and master content that you yourself might have just learned. The good news is that every time you teach something, you'll become more confident with the material, as well as your ability to teach it. You might also come to the realization that you don't know much about anything—until you have to teach it to others.

When you feel imposter syndrome creeping in, try these strategies (in no particular order).

- **Think about a past accomplishment:** Maybe even reflect on a time that you felt unprepared for the task at hand. What did you do, and how did it turn out? Chances are, you got through it and learned a lot. Whatever the outcome, it helped get you to where you are today.

- **Go next door:** Pop in to see a colleague you respect and let that person know how you're feeling. Ask how they deal with [*insert whatever you're feeling uneasy about*]. You'll probably find that you leave feeling a lot better than when you walked in.

- **Look into the future:** Think about how you're feeling now, and then think about how you want to feel a year, or several years, from now. The only way to get there is to go through it. Remember that every accomplished teacher has been where you've been, felt what you've felt, and gotten through it. You will, too!

- **Find a way to laugh:** When we laugh, we put things in perspective. Whether it's watching that video that always makes you smile or calling that friend who always makes you laugh, find something that redirects your angst and helps you remember that the job you do is also silly, funny, and wonderful.

Determine Necessary Classroom Procedures and Routines

While effective classroom management starts with you, it plays out each day in the many things that happen in your classroom. Teachers who effectively manage their classrooms don't have to repeatedly explain how they want students to do something; rather, they clearly and intentionally explain what they want done, give students an opportunity to practice it, and then make sure it continues to be done—knowing they might need to make adjustments along the way.

When it comes to managing your classroom, a *procedure* is what you want the students to do. A procedure becomes a *routine* when the students execute that procedure with automaticity or with just a little bit of prompting from you. For example, if you want all of your students to line up in a straight line outside your door each morning, that's a procedure. When the students start to line up each morning without you telling them that they need to, now that procedure is becoming a routine.

The ultimate goal of effective classroom management is to set up a system of procedures and routines where things run so smoothly that the management part seems almost invisible. Students know what they need to be doing and how to do it at all times. Of course, students are real people, and when real people are involved, things can get a bit tricky, so the following sections take you through some essential procedures and routines to make part of your classroom culture as well as some additional nice-to-have procedures and routines for you to consider adopting.

Essential Procedures

While this chapter explores several different types of procedures, and there are many more that might play out over the course of a single class period or an entire day, we find that the following five are critical to address with your students: (1) how class begins, (2) how the class quiets down, (3) how to ask for help or answer questions, (4) how to transition between tasks, and (5) how class ends.

How Class Begins

Setting a classroom procedure for how class begins is a straightforward process: What do you want students to do immediately upon entering the classroom? The most effective classroom managers don't need to give directions when that first bell rings, nor are students asking, "What should I do?" They are already working.

Clearly communicate with students how each day will begin in your class, what supplies they'll need (so they can get those supplies out in advance), and what they should begin working on. The beginning of class is a great time to have students complete something that they can do independently and successfully—this sets the tone that the work is important and the students can be successful. Some examples include the following.

- Working on a warmup (sometimes referred to as *bellwork*)
- Writing a few sentences in a journal about what they learned the previous day and what they think they're going to learn about today
- Reading (or rereading) about something that will be covered in class

This is also a great time to take attendance—the students will be quiet and engaged, and you can simply use your seating chart (as discussed in Use a Seating chart on page 8 in chapter 1) to see who is and isn't there. You'll be able to take attendance so quickly and quietly that students won't even realize it's happening.

It's also helpful to have an agenda for the day posted (have it in the same place each day) so the students can see exactly how the class or day will unfold. Rarely will students need to ask, "What are we doing?"

Tips to Thrive

Informally referred to by many teachers as the *number-one classroom management strategy* of all time, enthusiastically greeting students at the door sets the tone and pace for the entire class or day. If that sounds too good to be true, keep in mind that "In the classroom where the teacher greeted the students at the door, there was an increase in student engagement from 45 percent to 72 percent" (Allday, as cited in Wong & Wong, 2013). More recent research validates the claim that attentiveness and engagement increase when teachers use this strategy (Cook et al., 2018).

When you greet your students as they enter the classroom, you are immediately visible to them and are able to connect with them. It also shows that you are organized and ready for the day.

How Class Quiets Down

While a noisy classroom is very often an inevitable part of an active and engaged learning environment, there are times (lots of them) when you need to get the class quiet. Perhaps they've been engaged in an activity, and you need to give further directions. Or maybe they've just come in from lunch, and the energy in the room is running a little too high. Regardless of the reason, having clear and specific ways to quiet the room is a critical component of classroom management. When done well, the class quiets down quickly, and the learning moves forward smoothly. When not done well, it can be frustrating and result in having to beg and plead with your students over and over to be quiet (and that's not worth losing your voice over).

While there are many ways to quiet down your class, here are a few that work well (as long as you your students to respond to them).

- **Count down slowly from five:** Most every teacher has a routine for counting down from a noisy classroom to a quiet one. By the time you've made this countdown into a routine, a simple, "Please be silent in 5, 4, 3, 2, 1" is all it takes. When you get to 1, the class should be silent. The slow countdown gives students time to wrap up what they're saying, and at the same time, communicates an urgency that the class needs to be quiet within five seconds.

- **Use a fun rhyme or choral response:** Rhymes and choral responses are highly effective because they're easy to remember, easy to repeat (especially on command), and they sound great when everyone does them together. Some examples follow.

  - *Teacher*—"Class, class!"
  - *Students*—"Yes, yes!"
  - *Teacher*—"One, two, three . . . ."
  - Students—"Eyes on me!"

- **Raise your hand:** Establish for students that whenever they see your hand raised, it's time to stop talking and prompt their fellow students to stop talking as well.

There are many other ways to get a class quiet—and you'll find what works for you. What is most important is not which technique you use but *how* you teach students to follow this procedure (more on that later in this chapter).

How to Ask for Help or Answer Questions

In most school cultures, it is generally accepted that to ask for help or to answer a question that the teacher asks, a student raises their hand and waits to be called on. Of course, this is an assumption that we make as adults, and sometimes the students have other ideas. As teachers, sometimes we find ourselves needing to let go of our assumptions about what we think students should already know or were supposed to have learned in previous years and just get them the information that they need.

If you want students to raise their hand when they need help, clearly communicate this to them. Some teachers even use hand signals to communicate different things—such as one hand signal for when students need to use the restroom and another for when they need you to come over to them. This also saves you a lot of time because you won't need to have an entire conversation just for a student to use the restroom.

Does a student need to sharpen a pencil? Simply train students to hold up a pencil with the tip pointing upward. Then, when you deem it an appropriate time, all you need to do is point to the pencil and make a quick motion with your finger toward the pencil sharpener. The student can quickly sharpen the pencil and return to their seat. You just had an entire conversation with that student without saying a single word or breaking the flow of what you were doing.

How to Handle Transitions

Changing from one activity to another can be tricky and time-consuming, especially when students aren't sure what they should be doing (or if you're telling them what to do as they're doing it). Transitioning back to class after lunch or recess can also be a challenge, as it often requires a shift in students' physical, mental, and emotional energy, from the playground to the classroom.

The key to teaching students to transition is to *communicate everything in advance*. We dive into *how* to teach procedures later in this chapter, but here are some common examples of transitions that occur throughout the day.

- Entering the classroom to begin the period or day
- Changing from working independently into small groups and from working in small groups to working independently
- Moving from the carpet to desks and from desks to the carpet
- Anything that requires students to move or rearrange their desks
- Anything that requires students to take out or put away supplies and materials
- Exiting the classroom to end the period or day

When performed smoothly and correctly, effective transitions are a thing of beauty! They give students (especially the restless ones) an opportunity to move and stretch their bodies, and they can give you a quick moment to pause, take a breath, and prepare for whatever you have planned next.

How Class Ends

Also known as *dismissal*, the final moments before students leave your classroom is a critical procedure. Not only is it one final opportunity to say goodbye, it also sets the tone for how they show up the next day.

When that bell rings at the end of class, the procedure that you teach is the procedure that your students will follow. Do they clean up their desk and floor area and walk out calmly, or do they scream and run out of the classroom and into the hallways?

As teachers, we often get so focused on what we're teaching that we run out of time at the end of class. Then, we have to frantically wrap everything up quickly because the bell has rung. Be conscious of the time and try to begin your end-of-day procedures *before* the bell rings. You can even set an alarm or have a student remind you when there are only two minutes of class left.

Additional Procedures

Beyond the essential five procedures, many other procedures that happen throughout the day are important and help move things along efficiently. You'll develop these additional procedures through experience based on what you teach, your broader school culture, and so on, but here are just a few examples.

- **Leaving the classroom while the class is in progress:** It might not seem like something you need to discuss in advance with students, but it can be disruptive (and a bit weird) when a student just stands up in the middle of class and walks out. However, that student may just need to use the restroom. Some teachers instruct students to use a specific hand signal (such as holding up a fist) when they need to excuse themselves, and that allows the teacher to respond accordingly (sometimes with a corresponding hand signal, such as with an open hand, that let's the student know it's an OK time to leave). Discussing the procedure for leaving the classroom will save you time, confusion, and hopefully, accidents.

- **Note-taking:** There are a lot of interpretations of what it means to take notes. To some, note-taking means writing down or typing everything the teacher says. To others, it means a few scribbles of key points. And to still others, it means a few doodles and key words. If there is a specific way that you want students to take notes, teach them that format. Also keep in mind that effective note-taking is a skill that they will use in every class after yours, as well as throughout their lives.

- **Substitute teacher procedures:** As much as you plan, prepare, and take care of yourself, there will be mornings when you wake up and realize you're too sick or injured to go into school. (Don't stress it. Call in a substitute teacher and get some rest.) Your school might already have a template for teachers to use when they have a substitute. Regardless, make sure you include the following in your sub plans. Visit **go.SolutionTree.com/teacherefficacy** to download a free reproducible you can fill out with this and other helpful information, including those listed in the following bullets.

    ‣ A welcome letter, thanking the person for being there

    ‣ A lesson plan for the day

    ‣ Seating charts, bell schedule, and campus map

    ‣ Specific people and their phone or room numbers in case they need help throughout the day

    ‣ A form or place where they can report on how things went that day, including naming any students who were particularly helpful or unhelpful

    ‣ A few chocolate bars or other just-in-case items that get them through the day

- **Technology use:** Depending on the teaching setup in your classroom, your procedures might vary widely from another teacher's classroom. If your classroom has a cart where the technology is stored, you'll need to teach your students the procedure for checking out and turning in the devices, as well as how to plug them in, and so on. In addition, what do you want them to do once they get the device to their desk? Be as specific as possible with your expectations.

- **Emergency situations:** As educators, we will spend a lot of time preparing for a moment or instance that might never come. But should that moment come, everything we do in preparation will be 100 percent necessary. Whether it's a fire drill, active shooter drill, or any of the other possible emergency situations that we might encounter, it is critical that teachers and students know the exact procedures they are expected to follow. In most cases, your school already has a plan in place; practice that plan with seriousness and attention to detail, and ensure that every student understands what they need to do.

- **Food in the classroom:** Allowing students to eat in the classroom has both benefits (it's hard to learn when you're hungry) and drawbacks (are those ants?). If you decide not to allow food in your classroom, communicate this clearly. If you decide to allow food, it's critical that you communicate clearly with students exactly how you want it handled, including when and where they can eat, where you want them to throw away their trash (remember, ants), and how to clean off their desks when they are finished. This is especially important during extreme weather days when students might be staying in the classroom during lunch, recess, or both.

With effective procedures in place, your classroom will run smoother, with fewer distractions and misbehavior. You'll also find that students can get on task, stay on task, and complete tasks more quickly, helping you stress less and teach more each day.

Teach Classroom Procedures and Routines to Students

It's not enough to simply decide what classroom procedures and routines you want to have in place, you have to take time to effectively teach them to students. Only through careful and persistent cultivation of procedures will they become routines, ensuring that your class runs as smoothly as possible, as often as possible.

It's also important to *not* make assumptions that your students will arrive each day already knowing what you expect and what to do. We don't assume every student is going to arrive already knowing all of the academic content that they need to know to be successful in class, and we can approach classroom management the same way. Remember, students' previous teachers might have taught content differently (or not at all), or they might come from a home where behavioral expectations are different (or not taught at all). Your class is your opportunity to manage it in a way that works for both you and your students.

The following sections offer guidelines to help make sure everyone is on board.

- Plan ahead.
- Discuss why the procedure is important.

- Teach the procedure, then practice it.
- Understand that teaching procedures never ends.

Plan Ahead

The end of class is *not* the right time to talk about what to do at the end of class. And the middle of an activity where students are enthusiastically talking to each other is *not* the right time to teach them how to be quiet. Plan to teach the procedures *before* they are actually going to happen so that the students have time to practice, make corrections, and get it right.

When you first start teaching procedures, things will most likely take a bit longer than you expect. (Remember, this is also the first time your students will be learning about them from you and how you want things done.) As a general rule, plan on needing about twice as much time as you anticipate. If you think teaching students to walk in a straight line is going to take five minutes, you should probably plan on ten.

Of course, the best day to begin teaching procedures is the very first day of school, reinforcing these practices throughout the first few weeks. However, you might be reading this book after the beginning of the school year has already passed, so the second-best day to start is tomorrow! It's never too late to start implementing a new classroom procedure.

Keep in mind that it might take a few attempts, and in many cases, several attempts until students get it right. Because of that, planning ahead is critical. In addition, some students might seemingly master procedures quickly, while others need more time. And just because things go smoothly one day, doesn't mean that same procedure goes swimmingly the next. Planning ahead helps you acknowledge that there might be setbacks and make adjustments as you go.

Discuss Why the Procedure Is Important

Students aren't robots (no offense to robots), and they come to school each day searching for meaning in their friendships, their relationships with adults, and the content they are learning. Understanding how to follow procedures is an important part of being a student, as well as being a member of society. Have you ever gone to board an airline flight where one of the passengers isn't following the desired procedures? If you've flown, then you have, and you know it throws off the entire boarding procedure.

Before teaching the procedure itself, take a few moments to talk about the need for it with your students. Engage them by asking why they think a procedure might be important or how it might work most effectively. This gives them a sense of meaning and investment in the procedure and helps create a class culture where everyone works together. It moves a procedure from being about "just following some rule" to it being a foundational reason why everyone cooperates and expects the best from each other.

Here are a few examples of procedures you might teach and what you might say.

- **Walking in a line together from the playground to the classroom:** Say, "Each morning when the bell rings, we're going to walk together from our meeting spot on the playground to our classroom. It's important that we walk together in a quiet, straight line so that I can keep track of everyone in the class, everyone stays safe, and we don't disrupt any of the other classes. So let's talk about the procedure for walking together in a line . . . ."

- **Getting the class quiet after an activity:** Say, "There are going to be times when you are talking to each other during class, perhaps about something that we're learning. It's important that we're able to get quiet quickly so that I can give you more directions or so we can move on to something else. So, let's discuss the procedure for how we can all get quiet as quickly as possible . . . ."

- **A student needs to sharpen their pencil:** Say, "From time to time, you might need to sharpen your pencil. Of course, I want you to get it sharpened as quickly as possible, but it's important that when you get up to do it, there's no disruption to your learning or to the learning of your fellow students, so let me show you the procedure for when you need to sharpen your pencil . . . ."

Teach the Procedure, Then Practice It

After you discuss *why* the procedure is important, it's critical to give clear, step-by-step instructions on how you want things done. For example, when teaching students the procedure for how you want a class period to end, you could give the following directions.

> When you hear me say, "Let's go ahead and clean up," please make sure that you:
>
> Clean up everything that is on your desk and put it away either in your backpack or where it needs to go in the classroom.
>
> Check under your desk for any supplies or trash; if there's any trash, please pick it up and throw it away in the trash can next to the door on your way out. [Notice how placing the trash can next to the door is a classroom management strategy.]
>
> Sit quietly until I say, "See you tomorrow." When I do, please stand up and walk out quietly.

Of course, simply giving students the directions isn't enough. Give them some time to practice so that you can help them make any necessary corrections to master this procedure. For example, you might do this as an exercise during class or use the end-of-class experience for a time as a sort of live practice, knowing that it might take a few days or a week for students to understand your expectations of them. Be sure to show them some grace during the feeling-out period. When giving feedback, be as intentional and specific as possible. Instead of just saying, "Nice job," you could say, "I like the way everyone checked under their desks for trash—the next class is going to love walking into a room with a clean floor." And instead of saying, "We're not all walking properly in a straight line," you could say something more specific, such as "Please make sure to keep one arm's length away from the person in front of you, like we discussed."

Understand That Teaching Procedures Never Ends

As the year goes on, your students will get better and better at following procedures (to the point where they become well-honed routines), and you'll get better at teaching them. However, this doesn't mean everything is going to go well every day. There will even be days when things don't go well at all! Don't see this as a failure or a sudden loss of students' ability to follow a procedure; rather, view it as an opportunity to reteach it, reinforce it, or in some cases, scrap the procedure and start fresh with a new approach. Be flexible about your procedures, knowing that not every procedure you attempt to implement will work as well in practice as it does in your head. When you recognize that a procedure is unlikely to attain its intended goals, be humble and open to change. Students will recognize your desire to work *with* them and not just dictate *to* them.

There are also times of the year when classroom management becomes more challenging, especially around breaks, grading periods, and holidays. During these times, emotions among both students and teachers can run a bit higher than usual. February might be the shortest month on the calendar, but when it comes to managing your classroom, it is often the longest month of the school year. Even late-start days can prove extra challenging for some students, as their regular morning routines are disrupted, which can affect how they follow classroom procedures. Knowing and anticipating this in advance can serve as a good reminder that it's totally normal and that you might just need to plan a bit of extra time to review the procedures with your students.

Project Confidence

One of the most important aspects of your success as a teacher is the ability to maintain control of your classroom. Even on days when you're feeling less than sure about what you're doing, speaking confidently puts you in an excellent position to gain and maintain control of your classroom, and it will dramatically increase your ability to get and keep your students interested in what you're talking about. This doesn't mean you have to be fake or inauthentic. With each day, you'll step forward and grow into a more confident teacher.

These tips will help you get there.

- **Speak loudly:** Have you ever tried to watch a television show with the volume turned down too low? It can be a frustrating experience, and if you aren't able to increase the volume, you'll quickly get frustrated and lose interest. As a student, it's hard to stay engaged if you can't hear your teacher. There will be times when you increase your vocal volume and times when you will want to decrease it; however, when speaking to the entire class, make sure everyone can hear you. To do this, a great strategy is to find the person farthest away from you in the room and adjust your vocal volume so that they can hear you. Since they're the person sitting farthest from you, when they can hear you, everyone between you and that person should be able to hear you as well.

- **Speak clearly:** In many cases, the best way to make sure you are speaking clearly is to simply slow down. We often begin speaking too quickly when we are nervous or feel like we need to rush through the day's lesson to make sure we finish before the bell rings. Speaking slowly and clearly gives our students a much better chance to grasp the information—especially our students who are learning English and might need some additional time to think about and process what we're saying.

- **Stand confidently:** Although the number can vary, most communication experts agree that 70 to 93 percent of all communication is nonverbal (Advaney, 2017). This means that our posture, the way we move around our classroom, and our ability to make eye contact are critical factors in how we teach. When standing in front of your classroom, try to stand with your arms at your side and your shoulders back. Of course, there will be times when you stand with your arms crossed, but try not to get stuck in this position. When you walk, whether you are walking across your classroom or across your campus, walk with confidence. Walking, speaking, and standing with confidence send a clear message to your students that you are a confident teacher and that you show up each day to help grow confident students.

- **Move around:** One of the easiest ways to switch things up is to move around the classroom. You don't need to constantly pace back and forth or run circles around students. Casually walking from one side of the room to the other while you're talking forces students to shift how they are sitting and where they are looking, which helps to keep them engaged. It also helps keep *you* engaged, helps keep your energy up, and gives you the opportunity to see things from different angles and perspectives. You might also notice that students' posture changes as you come closer to them. Many will sit up as you get closer and relax a bit as you move farther away. This is good! It indicates that the students are engaged, aware of where you are, and following along.

- **Make eye contact:** Have you ever tried to have a face-to-face conversation with someone who wouldn't make eye contact with you? It can feel like they're not interested in you or the conversation (though it's important to keep neurological and cultural differences in mind). At the same time, when someone *is* making eye contact during a conversation, it's pretty hard to look away. While teaching, we're often having conversations with several people at the same time, so we can't maintain eye contact with just one person. However, we can maintain eye contact with the entire room. A quick eye-contact connection with each student can help everyone feel seen and valued—even if it's just for a quick moment.

As you look toward strategies to project confidence, it's important to be aware of how what you do and how you perceive student behavior must be filtered through the lens of culture. For example, while eye contact is an important social norm in U.S. culture, many cultures that your students may come from are different, and some cultures discourage eye contact.

To help mitigate this challenge, take a moment and discuss with your students how different cultures have different norms and expectations, and what the cultural expectations regarding eye contact are in your classroom. This could also be a great opportunity for you to learn more about your students' background while helping them feel comfortable and thrive in different environments.

Final Thoughts: Everything Matters

From greeting your students at the door to speaking confidently and mastering procedures and routines, effective classroom management is essential to establishing and sustaining a positive and orderly environment where everyone thrives. Not only does a well-managed class increase meaningful academic learning and facilitate social and emotional growth, it also decreases negative behaviors and increases the time students spend academically engaged (Gage & MacSuga-Gage, 2017; Oliver & Reschely, 2007).

Remember, some days will be better than others. On days where you struggle with classroom management, take the opportunity to share your struggles with your colleagues, asking them for advice. Or ask your principal who some of the most effective classroom managers are on your campus and see if you can pop in at some point to watch them teach.

When you manage your classroom successfully, it directly affects your students' ability to learn—and equally as important—your ability to teach effectively and love what you do.

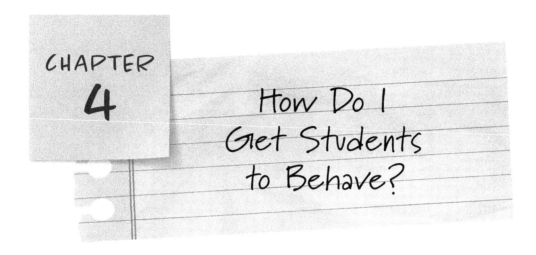

CHAPTER
4

How Do I Get Students to Behave?

There's a striking reality that hits every teacher in their first few weeks on the job: *every student is different.* Each day, students enter our classrooms with different dreams, goals, and ideas about how the world works. At the same time, they also enter our classrooms with different needs, experiences, and ways they react to how the world works. The obvious result: every student behaves differently.

As teachers, managing students' behavior can be quite a challenge, and at the same time, one of the greatest opportunities for growth (our students' *and* ours) and connection. While school is where students come to learn the academic skills they need to thrive in the world, it is also where we can help them build their self-awareness around how their behavior determines the strength of their relationships and the ability to be successful in many different situations.

In the first three chapters of this book, we explored how to set up your classroom, how to build relationships with students, and how to effectively manage your classroom. While this chapter specifically dives into behavior management, it is probably pretty clear that the more effort you put into these first three, the less effort you will need to put into managing student behavior.

In short, keep the following in mind.

- The more well-organized your physical classroom space is, the less likely students are to feel uncomfortable and overwhelmed, which is when many behavior issues arise.

- The stronger your relationships are with students, the less likely they are to feel disconnected, which is when many behavior issues arise.

- The more effectively you manage your classroom, the fewer opportunities students have to be off task or unclear about what they should be doing, which, once more, is when many behavior issues arise.

As a bonus item, and as you'll see in the chapter after this one, the more engaging and meaningful your lessons are, the less time your students will have to be off-task and misbehaving. And yet, despite all your best efforts, students are going to misbehave. That's where this chapter comes in.

Your ability to proactively and reactively respond to behavior challenges before and after they arise, and reframe them as learning opportunities, will go a long way toward developing the positive learning space that every teacher strives for. As mentioned in chapter 3 (page 31), Allday defines *behavior management* as the "techniques used by educators to promote appropriate behaviors and discourage inappropriate behaviors" (R. A. Allday, personal communication, October 27, 2015).

Behavior management can therefore be broken down into the following, which this chapter focuses on.

- Promote appropriate behaviors.
- Discourage inappropriate behaviors.

We follow our exploration of these topics with some additional strategies to help you succeed.

Promote Appropriate Behaviors

If you don't model what you expect, you'll come to expect what you model. Remember that the students are watching your every move, so it is imperative that your actions align with your message. A culture of "Do as I say, not as I do" won't cut it. We are helping students become adults who understand why the expectations are there. We do not serve them well if they believe that rules are imposed by adults and that they get to break the rules when they are older.

It's hard to insist that students show up on time and ready to learn if we ourselves aren't on time and ready to teach. It makes no sense to insist that students put away their phones if we are secretly (or not so secretly) checking ours between teaching moments. And when emotions run high, we can't tell a student to calm down if we ourselves are yelling.

Expectations are exactly what they sound like: they are *what you expect of your students*. But expectations are more than just what you want your students to do; they communicate your values and what is most important inside the world of your classroom and, ultimately, in the world far beyond it. Over the course of the school year, your students will live up to (or down to) whatever expectations you have of them—so set your expectations high!

As Tom Hierck (2017) suggests:

> Expectations serve as guidelines that are important not only in the classroom but, more often than not, also in life beyond the classroom's four walls. Expectations guide student responses academically and behaviorally. Expectations have an emphasis on

> lifelong learning and an eye toward growth. Rules, on the other hand, tend to be specific and are often responses to previous negative outcomes. Rules are attempts to guide student responses but tend to be reactionary and often do not bring about the desired change. (p. 20)

Framing the work of the classroom as expectations also avoids having to rush to deliver consequences that often accompany rules. As noted, setting expectations is more proactive, whereas enforcing rules tends to be more reactive. Your school might already have certain schoolwide expectations, and you can align your expectations with the overarching school expectations.

You create expectations two ways: (1) *for* your students or (2) *with* your students. Consider the following.

- Creating expectations *for* your students takes less time up front. Once you have determined what they are, be sure to communicate them clearly to your students and make them visible on a classroom poster where everyone can see them.

- Creating expectations *with* your students takes more time, as it requires an open and honest conversation with your students, but it helps students feel ownership of and investment in their environment. Regardless of their age, students have insightful thoughts about what should (and should not) happen in class. For example, the expectation of responsibility in kindergarten might be at the entry level and include things like *Listen to your teacher* or *Be kind*. At the high school level, this same expectation might align with *Complete all your work* or *Manage your time well*.

Regardless of how you arrive at your classroom expectations, here are three tips to make sure you maximize their effectiveness.

1. **Less is more:** While you might have several expectations that you've come up with, try boiling them down to between three and five. Having less than three might not cover as much as you need to, and having more than five can start to look like an exhaustive list of rules to the students, which not only lessens their importance but also makes them harder to follow, especially for elementary-age students.

2. **Keep expectations clear and simple:** Limit your expectations to one sentence, and make sure to write them using clear, simple wording that is age appropriate.

3. **Make expectations positive:** Write your expectations in a way that communicates the positive behavior that you *do* want to see, not the negative behavior that you don't. For example, saying "Arrive on time and prepared" communicates a positive expectation, as opposed to saying "Don't be late."

Figure 4.1 (page 48) is an example of expectations you could post on your wall.

Figure 4.1: Example classroom expectations.

When students live up to the expectations, let them know! Most people, regardless of their age, like to know when they're doing a good job at something. When you praise a student, be as specific as possible. Saying "Good job" is nice, but saying "I really like the way you walked in here on time and ready to go" communicates to that student exactly what they're doing right and encourages them to continue the specific behavior. This affects your work because not only does "increased use of praise directly [impact] student behavior by leading to more on-task behavior," but "teachers who use more positive feed-back develop supportive relationships with their students" (Pankonin & Myers, 2017).

The following strategies can help you promote appropriate behaviors.

- Use the positivity ratio.
- Remember trauma and the 254-day student.
- Let it go.

Using the Positivity Ratio

One possible answer comes in the form of a three-to-one positivity ratio (Fredrickson, 2009). For classroom purposes, this ratio stipulates that for every one negative emotion you share with a student (intentionally or unintentionally), it's important to balance it with three positive emotions. Barbara Fredrickson (2009) states this ratio is the tipping point at which a student will flourish (including being resilient to hard times) rather than languish. Once you start to incorporate the positivity principle in your classroom, you might also find that it starts to play out in all your interactions with your colleagues, parents and guardians, and other community members.

Think about all of the interactions you've had in your classroom over the last month. Would your analysis indicate that 75 percent of your interactions involved positive feedback rather than negative? If you've not yet started teaching, visit www.positivityratio. com/single.php for a quiz to audit yourself after your first month.

Many experienced teachers can recall the early struggles of trying to balance what our teacher training emphasizes (quiet, orderly classrooms as the optimal learning environment) with the realities of over thirty exuberant students and trying our best to use our outdoor voices to gain control of the room. It was a challenge to achieve a one-to-one positive-to-negative ratio, let alone trying to achieve the optimal levels described here. Achieving this ratio begins with a willingness to recognize what is currently occurring, followed by a desire to move toward the optimal positivity ratio. It's always interesting to work with a colleague to chart your interactions and see what your current positivity ratio is and use that as a helpful starting point.

It's also important that this not become an artificial activity. In other words, it can't simply be moments of panic as the class winds down and a teacher recalls making a negative comment and races to blurt out three positives before the class ends. Students notice a lack of sincerity and that would undermine the authentic effectiveness of this strategy.

Remembering Trauma and the 254-Day Student

We all get frustrated when working with a student who is not embracing what we often consider to be a basic request, even after we have taught it, practiced it, and most of the other students are on board with the desired behavior. It's even harder when we've tried a variety of strategies, like those in this chapter, and feel like we still haven't gotten through to the student. In truth, there can be good reasons for that: forming new habits (behaviors) is *hard* and it takes time.

Researchers Phillippa Lally, Cornelia van Jaarsveld, Henry Potts, and Jane Wardle (2009) looked at the process of habit formation in everyday life. The question of how long it takes to establish a new behavior is one every educator has likely pondered when working with a student exhibiting some very unique characteristics. The research offers both some comfort and some challenges. The time it took participants to have behaviors become automatic (learned and replicated when needed) ranged from 18 to 254 days (Lally et al., 2009). For educators, this means not every student gets it in the same way or time, and some will take even more than a traditional school year to make the behavior a habit of practice.

For some students, experiences with trauma can have a distinct effect on their ability and willingness to change their behaviors. Researchers Kathleen Fitzgerald Rice and Betsy McAlister Groves (2005) offer the following definition of *trauma*: "Trauma is an exceptional experience in which powerful and dangerous events overwhelm a person's capacity to cope" (p. 3). This definition includes words like *exceptional, powerful, dangerous*, and *overwhelm*, which should serve as a reminder that some of our students' lived experiences are well outside the boundaries of typical or healthy.

A more recent perspective on trauma defines it as "an emotional experience that directly impacts each student in a slightly different manner but has a definite and lasting impact on learning" (Eller & Hierck, 2021, page 15). This reminds educators of the uniqueness that accompanies trauma. What may be highly traumatic to one student may be on the low end of emotional impact for another. This does not imply a right/wrong dichotomy but does suggest that educators need to be aware of the unique impact of trauma on each student and their capacity to take up the lesson of the day.

According to learning expert Zaretta Hammond (2015), when children experience trauma, their brain may tell them to engage the fight, flight, hide, freeze, or fawn response. You may not be the source of the trauma, but the experience of that trauma may be causing the behaviors you are seeing. Interestingly, research finds that "Missing one opportunity to perform the behavior did not materially affect the habit formation process" (Lally, van Jaarsveld, Potts, & Wardle, 2009, as cited in Clear, n.d.). In other words, it doesn't matter if you mess up every now and then. Building better habits is not an all-or-nothing process.

However, repeating the behavior in a consistent context results in *automaticity*, which is when a specific behavior becomes an automatic, ingrained habit in response to a specific context or need. Consistency is important in this habit-forming process, and helping students identify what sparks a negative behavior is also helpful (Brier & Lanktree, 2013). For some students, this might be related to the activity (group work versus working alone), the subject matter (mathematics versus physical education), or the day of the week (Monday, after the weekend at home, versus Wednesday, when they have been back at school for a few days). Having students recognize what might be the trigger is the first step toward their ability to resolve the triggers and adopt a new replacement behavior. They also benefit from learning how to develop good behavior habits that help them get their needs met.

Letting It Go

As odd as it might seem to offer this as a strategy after an entire chapter on behavior management strategies, here it is: *sometimes, just let it go.* You don't have to respond to every misbehavior that happens. Trying to respond to everything will drive you toward your own unproductive behaviors, as it requires effort and energy that you just don't have (nobody does).

Whatever grade you teach, don't forget that there are disruptive behaviors that are naturally a part of that age. Kindergarteners are going to behave like kindergarteners, middle school students are going to behave like middle school students, and even high school seniors, who are about to enter the adult world, are going to behave like high school seniors. Find the humor where you can, marvel at the stories you'll have to tell, and remember that part of this wonderful profession of teaching means getting to meet and work with students who think and act completely different from anyone else.

Remember, even though you've discussed the expectations with the class and posted them on your wall, you can still modify, change, or rewrite them at any time. If you find a better way to communicate an expectation, or if something just isn't working, change it.

Discourage Inappropriate Behaviors

As we stated earlier, *every student behaves differently*. In addition, you will have students who behave wonderfully on some days; on other days, they'll make you want to pull your hair out. (We recommend you don't.) Some students need only to be corrected once; and of course, you'll have students who seem to need their behavior redirected repeatedly on a daily basis.

First, no matter how illogical or counterproductive a behavior may be, remember that students always have reasons for how they behave. They are constantly evolving beings who are still growing and learning to understand what they want and need and what kind of place they want to have in the world. The infinite number of variables that shape how they think and behave derive from experiences outside your classroom, and not all of those experiences are positive. Some of your most difficult students, behaviorally, are the ones who are in the most desperate need of some kind of positive adult influence in their lives. As you are forced to react to disruptive behaviors, never lose sight of this fact. Many educators are familiar with the notion of thinking of behavior as a form of communication. Shifting mindset and considering the purpose of a child's actions might lead educators to ask the critical question of why the student is using behaviors that are inconsistent with school.

Obviously, whatever motivations underpin a student's misbehavior, that doesn't mean that you can let it pass without action. So, your second need is to have a solid behavior-management plan in place. This will help you minimize misbehavior, redirect as needed, and keep everyone on track to learning. You have to know exactly what you will do when a student misbehaves, which means students also have to know what will happen, including what else will happen if the behavior continues.

The following sections offer strategies for determining the following.

- Know when to direct, correct, or connect.
- Know what to do when plan A doesn't work.
- Understand when to send students out of class.
- Recognize when students need their own plan.

Directing, Correcting, or Connecting

Remember that, above all, classrooms are a space for learning. An inability to meet the desired expectations may represent a skill gap, so using an instructional approach instead of rushing to consequences might be the best and easiest way to go. The following example identifies what the three approaches look like for Maria, who has a habit of calling out in class.

We have yet to meet a student who got "consequenced" to better behavior. Taking the approach that the student is in progress and working with them to develop the skills they need offers a better likelihood of success and potential growth. Breakthroughs happen when consequences are paired with instruction.

A strategy that helps teachers achieve the identified outcome is aligning instruction and remediation to the classroom's agreed-on expectations. Consider the Direct, Correct, Connect approach with a student like Maria, who is constantly shouting out answers instead of raising her hand to be called on:

> In the *direct* approach, the teacher simply tells the student what to do and indicates (or administers) the consequence. This threat does little to teach, and it's fairly easy to predict that a student like Maria will be receiving a consequence soon, as she has given repeated indicators that she does not currently possess the skills to meet the expectation in the context of a classroom. Let's be clear, this is not a question of whether or not Maria possesses the physical ability to raise her hand; it is about whether or not she possesses the behavioral skills to do it.

> In the *correct* approach, the teacher moves away from the rush to exacerbate the problem and toward the learning opportunity. The teacher reminds the student Maria of the desired outcome, lessening the threat of consequence. This seems to be a kinder, gentler approach to the issue and offers some strategy as a learning tool by reminding her of the expectation. However, there is still no connection to the bigger, desirable outcome.

> In the *connect* approach, the teacher is not thinking about consequences, but is totally immersed in the learning opportunity the shouting-out challenge presents. In this situation, the teacher intentionally connects the desired behavior to an important expectation in the classroom. The teacher reminds Maria of the need to exhibit the right behavior and provides an opportunity for her to demonstrate that she knows it. (Hierck, 2018, p. 117)

This approach mirrors what the early part of Tom's teaching career looked like. As a new teacher, Tom was convinced (and had frequent reminders in his teacher training) that the prime objective was to have the perfect learning environment, defined as an absolutely silent classroom. The mandate was to clamp down on any violation to this objective. Tom was, therefore, loud and quick to clamp down using (largely ineffective) consequences. This *direct* approach wasn't leading to the desired outcomes. Recognizing that it wasn't working, he thought the solution was to issue the consequence while also defining what the correct behavior was. This *correct* approach also did not alter, to any significant degree, the challenges he experienced. It took a while longer for Tom to realize that he needed to teach what he wanted to see—to *connect* the learning to the expectations. Remember this: you must teach it if you expect to see it.

Knowing What to Do When Plan A Doesn't Work

For many students, a verbal connect and correct will work to get their behavior back on track. But there is no one approach that will work with every student every time. So when plan A doesn't work out, the good news is that there are twenty-five more letters in the alphabet! Some students will require plan B, while others, plan C, and still others, well, you get the picture. The important thing is not to give up on any student who spends time in your classroom.

Regardless of how deep into the alphabet you go, it is important that you know what those steps are in advance and that the students know what they are as well. When you have a well-defined approach to behavior management, you can administer it without the students saying that it is unfair ("But you didn't do that for Javier!") and in a way that keeps you calm and grounded.

The steps you choose to take are ultimately your decision; however, be sure to see if there is already a schoolwide approach that you are expected to follow or incorporate into your plan. For example, some schools discourage you from sending a student to the office before you have tried (and documented) three actions.

Here are some examples of some steps teachers often use when students don't live up to behavior expectations.

- Issuing a verbal warning
- Conferencing with the student, often during recess or lunch
- Having student sit in another part of the classroom for a set time, often removed from other students (sometimes called a *time out* or a *refocus*)
- Making a phone call home to discuss the behavior with the student's parent or guardian
- Remembering that every day affords a fresh start
- Connecting students back to their previously demonstrated positive examples of behavior
- Listening to their story

When communicating and administering consequences, make sure to do so as calmly as possible. Even if you're burning up on the inside with anger and want to scream, remember that the goal is to help the student make better decisions in the future, not to shame and punish them. If you struggle with managing your own frustration and anger (it's OK if you do), it's vital that you have your own strategies for maintaining calm.

One approach we recommend is called the Five Senses Calming Strategy, and it's something you can use both for yourself and with your students. It comes from an educator in Woodridge, Illinois, named Dan Wolf, who creates and shares social-emotional learning tools that teachers can use to help students who struggle to behave within desired expectations (personal communication, October 30, 2023). This calming strategy can help both you and your students get grounded and refocus that negative energy in a more productive fashion. Use figure 4.2 as a tool or protocol when and where you find it's most needed. It can be helpful to use a piece of paper to write down answers to the prompts. You can also have the students complete the exercise on their own paper. Playing calm or reflective music during the activity will help the students relax and "turn on" their observational skills.

Directions: Use the following prompts to try to concentrate and identify things that may not be common or apparent.

See: Look for five things you can see. Try to see things around you that you may not have noticed in the past.

    1. _____

    2. _____

    3. _____

    4. _____

    5. _____

Feel: Notice four things you feel. Try to open up your thoughts and find things you feel that may be unique to you or not felt by others.

    1. _____

    2. _____

    3. _____

    4. _____

Hear: Listen and identify three things you can hear. Try to notice things you can hear that you may not have noticed in the past.

    1. _____

    2. _____

    3. _____

Smell: Notice two things you can smell. Try to write down smells that are subtle, like markers, paper, books, and so on.

    1. _____

    2. _____

Taste: Identify one thing you can taste. Try to pause and reflect on a taste that you have not noticed in the past.

    1. _____

Figure 4.2: Five Senses Calming strategy.

*Visit **go.SolutionTree.com/teacherefficacy** for a free reproducible version of this figure.*

Taking the time to process with yourself or with a student also has the added benefit of creating a reference point for future challenging moments. In other words, during the exact moment when you need to calm down or work with a student to calm down, you can simply say, "Let's do the five senses exercise." Then you or the student (or both of you together) can slip right into it without needing explanation.

Understanding When to Send Students Out of Class

There might be times when you'll feel like you have tried everything and that a student is making your class unteachable. It's always a tough call as to whether to send the student out of class, as many teachers feel that when you do, you are also sending out your ability to work with that student. There is also the fear that you're sending them out to an unsupervised situation. When you do need to send a student out of class, here are three options.

1. **Send them just outside of your reach and for just a short while:** You can say something like, "Sophia, I'm having a really hard time teaching class right now, and it seems like you might need to decompress. Please go stand outside the door, and I'll come check in with you in a few minutes."

2. **Send them to another teacher's classroom:** This, of course, requires that you and another teacher have communicated in advance and agree on the process for how this action works. That way, when your student arrives in their classroom, the other teacher knows why they are there and how to handle the situation. The receiving teacher is not there to add consequences and must remain neutral to the situation regarding the incoming student. However, they also do not have to endure any additional misbehavior.

3. **Send them to an administrator:** There may be times throughout the school year when options one and two aren't working or won't work. If a student becomes too difficult for you to manage, you need some help from a school administrator, such as a counselor, vice principal, or principal. Communicate ahead of time to the administrator that you may need to send a student to them in the near future. While sending them out of class to that office is an option, also consider calling the administrator to come remove the student from your classroom. This ensures that the student stays safe while it's happening. Recognize when options one and two aren't working.

Recognizing When Students Need Their Own Plan

Ever heard of the Pareto principle? Often referred to as the 80/20 rule, we see it play out in classrooms, where 20 percent of our collective students seem to provide 80 percent of our challenges in the classroom (Kruse, 2016). They are the students who are most challenging to connect with, to keep on task, and to help perform academically. They are the students who frustrate us, often to the point of exasperation. As mentioned previously in this chapter, they are also the students who need us the most.

Undesirable behavior is an indicator of an unmet need, not a character flaw: "Students don't act out because they are bad people. They are simply looking for ways to establish and maintain a sense of self while navigating through the sometimes extreme experiences they have" (Smith & Dearborn, 2016, p. 202).

Tips to Thrive

Remember that behavior is a form of communication! Instead of immediately reacting to a behavior, stop and ask yourself, "What is the student trying to communicate?" Addressing a student's needs can often be more effective (and less intense) than addressing the behavior they're exhibiting.

All teachers know they have a classroom full of unique individuals. It makes sense, then, to consider varied approaches depending on the student, the situation, the time of day, the day of the week, or other variables. And when putting together a behavior plan for a specific student, don't do it alone. Check in with teachers who are also teaching that student or who have taught them in prior years. What worked? What didn't? Check in with the school counselor or administrators to find out as much as you can about the student's life situation. And if possible, check in with the student's parent or guardian. And of course, meet with the student to discuss the behavior plan you are putting together so that it is something you create *with* them, instead of *for* them, or even worse, *to* them.

Keeping in mind that every student is different, remember that it's OK for some students to have different plans than the rest of the class. Effective behavior management isn't about getting every student the same thing; it's about getting every student what they need to be a successful member of your class.

Final Thoughts: That One Student

If it weren't for student behavior issues, our jobs as teachers would be a lot easier. Because of behavior issues, the work we do gets a lot more challenging, especially managing the behavior of an entire class. Every student behaves differently, and each year (or at least every few years), you'll encounter a student who, regardless of their age, will seem to have mastered the art of making it seemingly impossible to manage your classroom. The student will push all your buttons and make you question whether you chose the right profession, or whether you should stay in it.

That's the student who needs you the most.

This is the student who is crying out to be noticed, seen, and cared about. This is the student who shows up every day to see if you are going to accept them, support them, and believe in not just who they are but also who they can become. And when you look back on your time with that student, you'll realize that in your frustration, that's the student who helped you see how much you still had to learn and helped you grow into the teacher that you are.

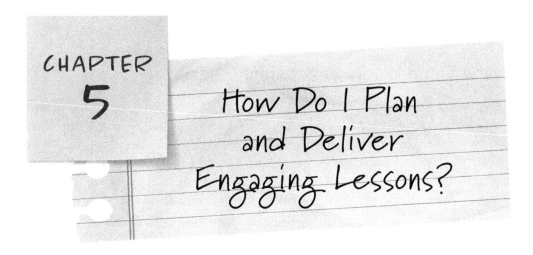

CHAPTER 5

How Do I Plan and Deliver Engaging Lessons?

We've all seen the sitcoms, memes, and video clips of the beyond-boring teacher who drones on and on from the front of the classroom while the students sit bored, motionless, and unengaged. It reminds us of the classic line from *Ferris Bueller's Day Off*: "Anyone . . . ? Anyone . . . ? Bueller . . . ?" (Hughes, 1986).

We've also all seen the Hollywood movies and television shows where the amazing teacher is defying all odds with their students, and every lesson plan they deliver is an Oscar-worthy performance where every word is perfectly placed and perfectly paced. Think of the late Robin Williams as maverick English teacher John Keating in *Dead Poets Society* (Weir, 1989): "I always thought the idea of education was to learn to think for yourself."

While there will probably be moments that feel like both extremes, the reality of what happens in your classroom will be somewhere in between. The tips and strategies in this chapter will help you plan and deliver lessons that get students interested, keep them engaged, and think about what they've learned long after they leave your classroom. For example, teaching a lesson on photosynthesis to thirty-five students who all show up with their own perspective, experience, and skill level can be a tough gig—it's also what makes teaching extremely exciting.

It's also important to acknowledge from the outset that teacher credential and training programs give you an abundance of templates and step-by-step instructions on how to create and deliver a lesson plan, so this chapter doesn't spend time doing that. Further, when it comes to lesson delivery, sometimes school administrators have a specific structure they want you and the other teachers to use to help keep things consistent across the school. So, instead of a pre-scripted plan, this chapter offers the following important guidance to consider for your lessons.

- Understand where engagement starts.
- Know the elements of an engaging lesson.
- Plan for how to wrap things up.

Ultimately, this chapter is devoted to helping you plan and deliver lessons that will get students engaged, keep them learning, and keep them coming back for more.

Understand Where Engagement Starts

When teachers think of engagement, it's akin to thinking about art—each person knows what they like, but it's hard to quantify it. In a broad sense, we all know that student engagement implies that students are so engaged in the learning that they don't want to disconnect from the pursuit. It speaks to the notion of persevering to the point where mastery is achieved and celebrated—students are giddy about accomplishing the learning target and have to share that accomplishment with others.

According to acclaimed education leader Phil Schlechty:

> The business of schools is to produce learning that is so compelling that students persist when they experience difficulties and that is so challenging that students have a sense of accomplishment, or satisfaction—indeed of delight, when they successfully accomplish the task assigned. (as cited in Erickson, 2005, page viii)

Let's be honest: there is no way a student is going to get excited about what you're teaching if you aren't excited about it yourself. This doesn't mean that you have to be Robin Williams playing John Keating in the movie *Dead Poets Society*. You don't have to jump around screaming and shouting about how amazing something is, but you do have to bring energy and enthusiasm to what you teach. Students of all ages can feel that energy about a topic, and their energy may match yours. Think about your own experiences as a student: were you enthusiastic about a topic that your teacher didn't seem interested in? At the same time, were you ever enthusiastic about something that the teacher was passionate about?

Keep in mind the importance of confidence that we discussed in the section Project Confidence (page 41 in chapter 3), and even when you're not feeling completely certain with what you are teaching: speak loudly, speak clearly, stand confidently, move around the classroom, and insist on eye contact (while having in mind that you may have students whose culture at home shuns eye contact). By projecting confidence, you make yourself engaging and automatically set up your lessons to be engaging as well.

Know the Elements of an Engaging Lesson

Engaging lessons guide students through several steps, and even some emotions, en route to learning the content. While every lesson might not contain every element discussed in the next part of this chapter, familiarizing yourself and being able to use them helps ensure that students with different learning styles get a chance to grasp the information. Plus, these options make the teaching and learning fun. You won't use all the elements in a single lesson; sometimes, you'll use more than others. And know that the more often you use the elements, the more familiar you'll become with them, and the better you'll be at using them.

Several elements compose an engaging lesson, each of which we explain in detail in the following sections.

- Build on what students already know.

- Be clear about what students will learn.

- Use a variety of teaching strategies.

- Ensure students can make real-world connections.

- Stop and check for understanding.

Build on What Students Already Know

Every student, in every subject, at every age, walks into our classroom already knowing something about the topics you're planning to teach—they just might not realize it yet! Unlocking what students already know, often referred to as *prior knowledge*, and using it as a springboard into the new content they will learn is an important strategy to get students engaged.

According to teacher Lauren Wenk (2017):

> Our students come to us each with their own prior knowledge, conceptual understanding, skills and beliefs. When we present them with problems or new information, their prior knowledge and experiences influence their thinking. Each student might understand what we say in slightly different ways—attending to different aspects of the question, interpreting and responding differently to the learning environment, etc.—all of which significantly affects their abilities to solve the problems we present, to reason, and to acquire new knowledge.
>
> New learning is constructed on prior knowledge. The more we understand about what students already think, and the more we help them engage their prior understandings, the more likely they are to learn well—and the less likely they are to misinterpret the material in our courses.

The following sections offer three easy and effective ways to unlock students' prior knowledge and get them buzzing about what's to come: (1) just ask, (2) picture prediction, and (3) previously on.

Just Ask

According to the habits of mind researchers Arthur L. Costa and Bena Kallick (2000), "Careful, intentional and mindful questioning is one of the most powerful tools a skillful teacher possesses" (p. 34). When we ask a student a thoughtful question, it forces them to stop, reflect, and come up with an answer that helps them learn and remember what they've learned. Of course, when teachers connect those questions with the need to activate what students already know in an effort to set up students for the learning they'll do, asking good questions serves as an important strategy that empowers students to learn and grow.

Suppose you're going to begin a unit on World War II. You can start by asking your class some questions that will lead up to that topic. Keeping in mind that some students will already have some knowledge of World War II and others will have very little, you can design your questions so that everyone in the class can engage. For example, you could ask a series of three questions.

1. What do you know about war? (This is a good general question to spark some thinking.)

2. Do you know anyone who has been affected by a war or fought in one? (This question starts to get students thinking about their own lives and experiences and those of people they know.)

3. Have you ever heard of the Holocaust? (With this question, you're giving a preview of what's to come while assessing what knowledge students already have about the topic you're going to cover.)

Keep in mind that the purpose of these questions is to connect what students already know to what they are about to learn—don't let yourself and the class get stuck for too long discussing a question. Remember, the purpose is to spark prior knowledge so you can get on to the lesson.

There are a variety of ways that you can ask these questions. You could start with the standard whole group. You could also utilize the think-pair-share strategy, posing a question, giving students a short amount of time to think about their answer on their own (*think*), then turning to a partner to discuss their thoughts together (*pair*), then having them share aloud with the rest of the class (*share*). Or, you could have them answer the question via a writing prompt, which they do on their own. Don't limit yourself to only these ideas. Look for and try many ways to get students answering your questions.

Picture Prediction

Picture prediction is super simple and effective. Find a picture of something that represents the topic you will cover and put up a picture of it for students to see. Then, simply ask one (or both) of the following questions.

- What do you think we're going to be learning about today?
- What words or phrases do you think we are going to be using?

Make a class list of student responses, have students write them down, or enter them into an app the class uses. It can be fun for the students to look back on what they predicted the lesson was going to be about versus what the lesson was actually on.

Picture prediction is a great way to spark interest and also expose students to new vocabulary, as their classmates will be offering words and phrases that they haven't yet heard.

Previously On

Have you ever watched a television series, and from the second episode on, it starts with a "previously on" refresher? It immediately sucks you in by reminding you of what you've previously seen (there's that previous knowledge) and prepares you for what's to come. We can do the same in our classrooms.

Even though you may have just discussed something yesterday, remember that since then, students have attended other classes, or you may have covered a multitude of additional topics as part of other lessons. They've also gone home and had additional experiences outside of school. It can seem like they don't remember what was discussed just yesterday, but what they really need is a quick refresher.

It can be as simple as saying, "Previously in [insert your name]'s class, we . . . ." Then, take a moment to tell the students some key aspects of what you covered. It also helps to show them any pictures, objects, or reminders that might spark a memory of what they've already learned. Of course, after you start with a good "Previously on," you'll probably want to consider ending the class with a "Next time on," because who doesn't love a good cliff-hanger?

Tips to Thrive

Remember that as the teacher, *you* set the tone for how students are going to feel about their learning. A fun way to do that is to take on the attitude of, "Either way, that's *great*!" If a student indicates that they have some background knowledge about a topic, you can say, "That's *great*! This is going to be an opportunity for you to build on that knowledge and learn even more." If a student indicates that they don't think they have any background knowledge about a topic, you can say: "That's *great*! This is going to be an opportunity for you to learn some new things about the world and your life."

Be Clear About What Students Will Learn

Start by asking yourself, "By the time my students leave my class today, what do I want them to be able to do?" Do you want them to add fractions with unlike denominators? Or perhaps you want them to identify the causes of global warming? Maybe it's starting new sentences with a capital letter? Whatever your objective or learning targets are, be as specific as possible in describing them to students, using age-appropriate language. Being clear about what students will learn will help them do exactly that—learn! Here are three tips to help you identify exactly what you want students to learn.

1. Use your academic standards.
2. Break it down.
3. Post it, say it, remind it.

Use Your Academic Standards

Just about every school has a set of academic standards, a list (usually a pretty long one) of predetermined skills and topics that students should learn in every class, subject, and grade. These might be national standards, state- or province-level standards, or even standards dictated by the school district. While there is sometimes political controversy about which standards should and should not be included, it's important to know and understand the standards for your school, grade, and class because they tell you exactly what you'll need to cover. Many schools and districts make pacing guides to help teachers get through all of the standards by the end of the school year. In many schools, collaborative teacher teams work together to determine how to prioritize and teach standards to ensure a guaranteed and viable curriculum (DuFour, DuFour, Eaker, Many, & Mattos, 2016). In any case, pacing guides map out what to cover and how long to spend on each standard (some require more time than others). Before you start writing lessons, be sure to get a copy of the state standards for each class you'll be teaching and ask if a pacing guide has already been made.

Break It Down

Sometimes there is a lot of information contained in one standard. Remember, you don't need to teach everything all at once. Have you ever bought a piece of furniture, then brought it home and realized it needed to be assembled? Hopefully, you used the provided directions that took you through it step by step. Of course, even though you followed the directions carefully, that furniture might still be a bit wobbly—that's OK, we'll cover how to deal with that in the assessment chapter.

This calls back to our previous reference to learning targets. As an individual teacher or as part of a collaborative team, it's critical to be able to break down a standard into pieces that make up the desired learning outcomes for a lesson (DuFour et al., 2016). Also called *chunking*, this is an important way to help students learn one step or one piece at a time. When conveying these learning targets or chunks to students, Rick Stiggins (2004) recommends using a series of *I can* statements that are grade-level appropriate. For example, "I can write a complete sentence," or, "I can explain how gravity affects an object."

Post It, Say It, Remind It

One of the best things a student can say as they enter your classroom is "What are we doing today?" This question shows they're interested and engaged, and as such, it deserves a good answer. As the teacher, it's a fantastic opportunity to enthusiastically say, "Today we're going to learn about a 16th-century poet who told crazy stories about people in high-drama relationships." (We really wish just one of our high school English teachers had described Shakespeare that way.)

Then, on the board under Objective, you have written "Analyze the impact of specific word choices on meaning and tone," which you've already posted on your board, and now point out to the students at the beginning of the lesson. You can also say, "By the time you leave today, you're going to be able to understand how the specific words authors use change the meaning and tone of what they're saying" (California Department of Education, 2013), just like all of us sometimes use different tones to get our points across. The more clearly you can describe a standard or learning target in simple, student-friendly language, the more open students will be to learning about it.

Throughout the lesson (especially at the end), remind students of the day's objective and point out their progress toward mastering it. Many school administrators will require you to write your daily objective on the board or have it posted. Often, it's a school policy. Even if they don't, having your objective visible is a great idea that not only provides clarity for students about what they must learn but also helps keep you focused on what you need to teach!

Tips to Thrive

When being interviewed about what she wishes she had known before starting teaching, one teacher summed up the need to be flexible perfectly:

> Lesson plans can change the hour before class starts, or you only might be able to get through half of a lesson because something unexpected happened in class, or you realize too late that the kids really aren't ready to move on to the next activity. It's easy to get frustrated with that, but part of what I find is helpful to be an effective teacher is to just take a deep breath and realize that the days never really go as you carefully planned. (as cited in Gillett, 2016)

Use a Variety of Teaching Strategies

Think for a moment about the phrase *boring lecture*. What makes it so boring? Most likely, you're envisioning a teacher standing in front of a class (maybe even behind a podium) the entire time, speaking in a monotone voice, and showing presentation slides filled with text while the audience sits motionless. Many educators refer to this as sit-and-get instruction, though it's more accurately thought of as *direct instruction*. And make no mistake, direct instruction has its place in your teaching playbook, but if that's all you have to offer students, no matter how charming you are, you won't keep your students engaged.

An important thing to recognize about students is that they don't all gravitate to one specific form of instruction or another. Often referred to as *cognitive processing styles*, it recognizes that there are different ways that individuals think, perceive, and remember information—in short, how someone prefers to process information. In *Doable Differentiation: 12 Strategies to Meet the Needs of All Learners*, Jane A. G. Kise (2021) refers to four cognitive processing styles according to what students typically gravitate toward.

1. Structure and certainty (*Let me know what to do*)

2. Experience and movement (*Let me do something*)

3. Vision and interpretation (*Let me follow my own lead*)

4. Question and connection (*Let me lead as I learn*)

Kise contends that teachers need not cater every lesson to every style (students must also learn to learn in multiple ways), but that it's important to ensure units cater to each style at some point.

Thus, using a variety of teaching strategies means mixing it up when it comes to how you deliver a lesson. For example, mixing it up could include any combination of the following.

- Have students talk to each other about the material (this could be with partners or in small or large groups).

- Have students do some writing about what they're learning.

- Get students moving around or somehow using their bodies.

- Give students some time to work on their own.

- Organize a learning game to be played in small or large groups.

- Incorporate music or other audio-visual content into a lesson.

Obviously, there are many more strategies, and you don't need to try to fit them all in during a single lesson. Over the course of your career, you'll learn a variety of specific strategies that you'll trust yourself to use effectively with students in specific contexts. But even as you evolve into a crafty veteran teacher, make sure you're always on the lookout for new strategies and continually mix it up not just for your students, but for you as well!

Ensure Students Can Make Real-World Connections

Sometimes it's easy to get so focused on *what* we're teaching that we often forget about *why* we're teaching it. Staying conscious about why students need to learn something is a critical component to how well they'll learn the material and how engaged they'll be while learning it (Mendler, 2014). Just as sales professionals always connect the products they're selling with an answer to the customer's question, "What's in it for me?" teachers can do the same. The difference is that our product is knowledge.

Part of making content real for students is to connect it not just to the world they live in, but the world they know (*their* world). When a student asks, "What does this have to do with me?" you should be able to answer that question. When a student asks, "When am I ever going to use this?" you should be able to answer that one, too.

Even better, if you can explain the answer to either of the preceding questions to students *before* they ask, you'll greatly improve the students' interest level (Roberto, 2021). To help you answer your students' questions about real-world connections before they ask them, here are four questions you can ask yourself.

- What is happening in my students' lives right now that I can connect to what I'm teaching?

- What are my students interested in that I can connect to what I'm teaching?

- What have we already covered in class, or what are we going to cover, that I can connect to what I'm teaching?

- What skills will my students need to be successful throughout their lives, and how can what I'm teaching help them gain those skills?

You don't need to spend a lot of time coming up with these real-world connections. Sometimes just a quick mention is enough to get students on board and understand why they need to learn what you've got for them.

Stop and Check for Understanding

There will be times during a lesson or at the end of a lesson when you look up and see a look of complete confusion on some (or all) of your students' faces. This is totally normal, and it's great information for you to respond to. There will also be times when students are grasping the information, making clear connections, and excited for more. Believe it or not, these little checks for understanding are powerful forms of formative assessment, which we cover more specifically in chapter 6 (page 69). For now, just know that stopping at various points along your lesson to check for understanding is a great way to make sure your students are following along and prevents leaving some students lost or otherwise disengaged while you and the rest of the class roar ahead.

And of course, there will be moments when a lesson is going badly. Don't be afraid to hit pause on the lesson and rethink it. It might be helpful to think of teaching a lesson-going-badly like trying to ride a bike with a flat tire. Sure, you might get there eventually, but taking a moment to stop, get off the bike, and pump up the tire will help you get back on track and let you soar past where you would have been if you were still riding with the flat.

Consider this, from education author Cynthia Thomas (n.d.):

> Even if you have planned a lesson and have a clear goal in mind, if your approach is not working—for whatever reason—stop! Regroup and start over with a different approach, or abandon your planned lesson entirely and go on to something else. At the end of the day, be honest with yourself as you examine what went wrong and make plans for the next day.

Here are a few easy ways to check for understanding throughout a lesson without slowing it down too much.

- **Ask a question about what you've just been covering:** You'll be able to gauge your students' level of understanding by some of the responses they give. Confused, shaky responses could indicate that you might need to back up a bit or slow down. Just make sure you ask a variety of students—not just the ones who always seem to know the answers. At the same time, be conscious that you're not repeatedly asking questions of students you know struggle with the content, which could lead to them feeling picked on.

- **Have them stop and write:** A great way to check for understanding is to have students take a few minutes (or even less) to write down (or type) something that they've learned so far. Just a quick sentence or phrase is enough, and at the end of the day, they'll have a running record of several things they've learned (especially if you do it more than once during a class). You can even give this activity a cool name, such as Pencil Pause or Thought Jot. You can also use these as exit tickets, which we discuss in the next section.

- **Feel the vibe:** As teachers, sometimes one of the most important things we can do is simply feel the vibe in our classroom. There's no step-by-step for this; you just need to develop and trust your instincts, and grab an honest feeling about how the lesson is going. If there seems to be a quiet, confused vibe among your students, you can make adjustments by backing up a bit. If the vibe seems chaotic and disorganized, you can slow things down and adjust accordingly. If there's a vibe that things are going great and everyone is learning—then, full steam ahead!

Plan for How to Wrap Things Up

Just as an engaging lesson opens with utilizing students' background knowledge, it ends with shining a spotlight on what students have learned. When you understand what you've learned, you also realize that the time you spent in class was totally worth it. Giving a lesson closure gives everyone a chance to reflect on what they've learned, get any remaining questions answered (or at least submitted so you can return to them the next day), and maybe even get excited about what the next class will bring.

Sometimes wrapping up a lesson and giving it closure is one of the most difficult parts of teaching a lesson. Why? Because we run out of time. Maybe you didn't get through everything you wanted to get through; maybe you got a bit sidetracked by announcements over the loudspeaker, or perhaps a disruptive student cost you a chunk of instruction time. All of these will happen at some point, but whenever possible, try to build in some time for students to reflect on what they've just learned. Exit tickets and learning journals are a couple of easy ways to bring closure to the lesson.

Exit Tickets

On a sticky note or a small scrap of paper, have students write something they've learned that day or type it into whatever app your class uses. If time permits, you can spend some time having them share what they wrote with each other. On their way out of the classroom, they can stick the notes on the wall or place the scrap of paper in a basket. The next day, you can use these notes to remind the class what they learned yesterday and activate that prior knowledge.

Learning Journals

Learning journals are an easy way for students to keep a running record of what they have learned. If at the end of each class (or whatever frequency you want to use) they are recording what they've learned, by the end of the week, month, or semester they'll have amassed quite the record of all they've done and be amazed at all they've learned. Journals can also be done using video—where students do a quick recording talking to the camera about what they've learned. Whether it's in their own handwriting, typing it into an online journal, drawing pictures that represent the learning, recording videos, or any other idea, you can provide students an opportunity to choose what works best for them. You might also offer options to journal individually, or in small or large groups. Again, mix it up!

Tips to Thrive

The suggestions in this section don't need to be limited to focusing on what students just learned. Empower students to use this wrap-up time to ask (or send you) questions they still have, identify where they're still confused, or anything else you think is important to address.

Final Thoughts: Evolve, Improve, and Stay Flexible

As teachers, the lessons we deliver are the visible product that we share with the world. It's where our planning, relationship building, classroom management, and everything else that we cover in this book come together to help students learn the content they need to know to be successful throughout their lives.

Some days your lessons go well, and you leave school feeling like you are on top of the world. There are also days when your lessons do *not* go well, and you'll feel defeated and disappointed. Many days, you'll be somewhere in between, and you'll leave the classroom feeling like your lessons are just OK. In all three cases, know that you are not alone. Pay attention to what worked, what didn't, and where you can improve upon the lesson. Over time, you'll teach those lessons again—and as you continually tweak and improve them, they'll get better each time.

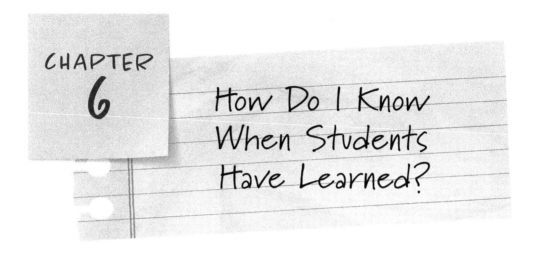

CHAPTER 6

How Do I Know When Students Have Learned?

Every teacher is expected to design lessons that are engaging and inspiring. We also suspect that every teacher designs these lessons with an eye toward all students learning and achieving the desired outcomes.

Despite those two givens, many questions remain. How do you know when your students have mastered the content? What are you prepared to do if they have not mastered the key content? Why assess students' progress?

This last question is one all educators should ask. It may, in fact, be the key question. The question leads educators to think about their assessment practice. How do they glean information about student progress? How do they know if student understanding is progressing? If the purpose is to focus on student learning—and ideally, it is—then educators must plan their current assessment practice, instruction, scaffolding, differentiation, interventions, and remediation to align with that desired outcome. To that end, this chapter helps you do the following.

- Understand the purpose of formative assessment.
- Understand the purpose of summative assessments and student mastery.
- Understand the purpose of grading.
- Offer second chances.
- Plan interventions driven by evidence.

Understand the Purpose of Formative Assessment

For those new to the profession, your connection to the conversation about formative assessment during your training might have been more theoretical than the practical pieces you encountered once you started with your own teaching assignment. If you type the words *formative assessment* into a Google search, hundreds of thousands of items are identified. It is perhaps because of these many ideas and interpretations about what makes for an effective formative assessment that the practice is still confusing and unevenly applied within districts, schools, departments, and classrooms. Given this real-ity, let's look at a few interpretations of formative assessment.

At the most basic level, the Glossary of Education Reform (2014) defines *formative assessment* as follows:

> Formative assessments help teachers identify concepts that students are struggling to understand, skills they are having difficulty acquiring, or learning [targets] they have not yet achieved so that adjustments can be made to lessons, instructional techniques, and academic support. The general goal of formative assessment is to collect detailed information that can be used to improve instruction and student learning *while it's happening*. What makes an assessment "formative" is not the design . . . but the way it is used—i.e., to inform in-process teaching and learning modifications. [Italics in original]

This quote reminds teachers about the need to regularly check on the learning their students are experiencing. These frequent checks not only inform the teacher about the effectiveness of their instruction and delivery but also inform students about their prog-ress toward proficiency on the learning targets. The sooner you gather and share the information, the smaller the learning gap, and the easier it becomes to intervene and close that gap.

One of the most widely accepted interpretations of formative classroom practice comes from education experts Paul Black and Dylan Wiliam, who authored a landmark paper in 1998 on its merits called "Inside the Black Box: Raising Standards Through Classroom Assessment." In the paper, they argue that "formative assessment is an essential compo-nent of classroom work and raises student achievement" (Black & Wiliam, 1998). Later, they would say of formative practices:

> Practice in a classroom is formative to the extent that evidence about student achievement is elicited, interpreted, and used by teachers, learners, or peers, to make decisions about the next steps in instruction that are likely to be better, or better founded, than the decisions they would have taken in the absence of the evidence that was elicited. (Black & Wiliam, 2009, p. 9)

Ultimately, as Tom Hierck and Angie Freese (2018) state, formative assessment is a tool that empowers educators to "monitor student learning on a timely basis, which provides more discrete feedback on which concepts are secure, which concepts need more support, and what misconceptions or errors are present so that corrective instruction can occur" (p. 62). In essence, teachers design formative assessments to assess the key learning out-comes of the priority standards or essential learning targets.

Hierck and Freese (2018) identify three criteria that make formative assessments ben-eficial and produce positive outcomes.

1. If a student achieves a proficient score, that score must accurately indicate that a student has learned what was intended.

2. If a student's score shows a lack of proficiency (a *not-yet score*), that score should clearly and specifically indicate that the student needs additional support.

3. When educators analyze data from formative assessments and look at the errors students made, they must use those errors to efficiently determine student needs and target intervention.

One final point to consider when discussing formative assessments is housed in the word *formative*. These assessments are designed to inform, and therefore should never appear as a permanent grade in your gradebook. The term is not based on when the assessment occurs (early in a unit) or a label you attach to it (practice) but reflects how you use the evidence gathered. Every grade assigned to a student is summative (as detailed later in this chapter) if it cannot be altered. There is no formula to determine a final grade that suggests a percentage for formative and a percentage for summative. All grades, if unalterable, are 100 percent summative.

Renowned assessment experts Kim Bailey and Chris Jakicic (2023) have a second edition of their great book on formative assessment, *Common Formative Assessment*, and they provide a handy protocol for teachers to use when they create formative assessments (see figure 6.1, page 72).

Note that this protocol was designed for use among members of a collaborative teacher team as part of a schoolwide professional learning community (PLC). While we included only the seven-step process here, Bailey & Jakicic (2023) offer additional insight and guidance for following these steps as part of a team. If you are fortunate enough to work as part of a collaborative team, especially in a PLC context, we highly recommend their superb resource for improving your team's formative assessment practices.

Understand the Purpose of Summative Assessment and Student Mastery

If formative assessment is to indicate progress and growth, how will teachers indicate that a student has mastered the desired learning outcomes? The answer comes in the form of summative assessment. While many of the same criteria for creating assessments may be as similar for summative assessments as they are for formative assessments, how you use the evidence the assessment generates is different. As mentioned in the previous section, formative assessments inform the next steps in the teaching and learning cycle. Summative assessments evaluate student learning at the end of a teaching unit by measuring results against a standard or external benchmark.

Summative assessments measure what students have learned as of a certain period of time. An often-used analogy to compare formative and summative is that formative is akin to the cook tasting the soup, while summative is akin to the customer tasting the

Facilitator Notes

Remind team members that the purpose of each common formative assessment is to provide data back to the team about which students have or have not mastered each of the learning targets being assessed. The assessment needs to be short and easy enough to score so that the team can respond quickly to the results.

The team will respond to students who need additional time and support around a specific learning target, those who might benefit from additional practice, and those who would benefit from opportunities for enrichment and extension.

Materials Needed

- The unwrapped standard
- The template for the assessment plan

The Design Process

Step One: Decide What to Assess

Unwrapping is the process through which a team identifies the smaller skills and concepts, or learning targets, needed to reach the performance expectations of the essential standard. Consider all the learning targets you have found during the unwrapping process that are being taught during this part of the unit. Decide which of these targets to assess. Remember you do not have to assess every learning target.

Consider:

1. Which targets are most likely to cause certain students difficulty?
2. Which targets are most important or prerequisite skills for information to come later in this unit?
3. Which targets are absolutely necessary for students to know?

Step Two: Decide How to Assess

For each learning target, make sure team members agree on the expected level of thinking for mastery of that target. For each learning target, choose the most appropriate assessment method: selected response, constructed response, or performance assessment. Make sure that the thinking level you're expecting can be assessed with the type of assessment you've chosen.

Step Three: Develop the Assessment Plan

Complete the assessment plan. Decide what type of items and how many items you will use to assess student learning on each target. Consider how long the assessment will take to administer and how much time teachers will need to score the results.

Step Four: Determine the Timeline

Decide the date or range of dates for administering the assessment and the date for the next meeting to discuss results. Remember to consider scoring time before establishing the date for the meeting to discuss the data.

Step Five: Write the Assessment

Use the guidelines for quality item writing while writing the assessment.

Step Six: Review the Assessment Before Administration

Review the assessment to make sure that the directions are clear and that students will understand what you are expecting from them during the assessment.

Step Seven: Set Proficiency Criteria and Decide How to Gather the Data

Determine what the score for proficiency will be so that data can be reported back by learning target and by student.

Source: Adapted from Bailey & Jakicic, 2023, p. 82.

Figure 6.1: Sample protocol for developing a formative assessment.

soup. The cook may still be able to adjust based on criteria important in the creation of a great bowl of soup—a formative opportunity. The cook can intervene no further once the soup goes out to the customer, who will give the final grade on the soup—summative and based on established criteria. Although, technically, a teacher *can* still intervene if a student does not demonstrate proficiency on a summative assessment. (In that case, this makes the assessment formative. Any time an assessment result can be replaced by an improved performance, the assessment is formative.) At this point, however, it's the difference between the cook making adjustments while in the kitchen versus going back to the drawing board to make a whole new batch of soup for the customer.

Ultimately, because the data are actionable, all assessment data tell teachers what to do next. Teachers must be responsive to the evidence they have from the assessment. The focus has to be on student results, not teacher intentions. Teachers can't:

> limit assessment analysis to determining what's *wrong with students*. [They] must use the evidence of student learning to collaborate with colleagues to identify either teaching strengths to share, or areas of concern for which to seek new instructional strategies. The purposes of assessment ought to be framed around diagnosing student learning difficulties and setting individual teacher, and team goals for student improvement. (Hierck, 2016)

Table 6.1 offers some examples of what might constitute formative and summative assessments.

Table 6.1: Formative and Summative Assessment Types

Formative	Summative
• Brief reflection writing • Class discussions • Exit tickets • Low-stakes group work • Quizzes • Surveys	• Standardized tests • Final exams • Final essays • Final presentations • Final projects • Final reports

One final piece of information that needs to be considered is that the question of formative and summative is not an either/or proposition. Teachers should strive for a balance of the two, while recognizing that the emphasis on practice (formative) should yield better results in the game (summative).

Understand the Purpose of Grading

Grading may well be one of the most controversial issues you will face as a teacher. The topic inspires more emotion on all sides of the question than almost any other in our profession. The phrase *psychologically harmful* is sometimes used to describe the results grades have on students (Kohn, 1999); other experts question the integrity of the A–F system and cite well-documented trends in grade inflation (Rojstaczer & Healy, 2012). Grading is fraught with challenges born out of perceived fairness, inequities, practice, and standardization. Oftentimes, teachers arrive at a school that has fairly defined systemic expectations around grades and grading already in place. Even in those circumstances, however, you have to know how to make sense of it all.

Your journey begins by ensuring you understand what it means to grade student work. Just as with formative and summative assessment, you have to know what your grading system is meant to accomplish. Yes, it is primarily a way to evaluate student work. You can also use it as a vehicle to provide feedback. This feedback may indicate the current performance level, or it may be a step in the process of revision as a student works toward proficiency. But implemented appropriately, grades can do much more. A grade can help you see what information, concepts, and skills students have proficiency with and where proficiency has not yet been achieved. They also help you communicate student performance to third parties, including parents and guardians, administrators, school boards, and post-secondary institutions.

Definitions are plentiful, but with so many stakeholders involved, perhaps it's not at all surprising that the practice and policy surrounding grading and reporting drive many conversations in schools, perhaps generating more emotion and resistance to change than any other topic in our profession. So, if definitions don't offer much clarity, how can teachers move forward and incorporate the essentials of effective grading practice? More importantly, when data-informed evidence suggests that we evolve or change our grading practices, how do we react to the inevitable resistance change incurs?

This is not to suggest that every recollection of grading is entirely negative. We've had many instances of colleagues sharing recollections of receiving positive affirmation through grades. But as we hear many of those same colleagues recall some overt negative experiences, we're left wondering what may have happened to those students who didn't have the support or resilience to overcome the negative evaluation of their skills or progress. Educator and author Thomas R. Guskey (2015) suggests, "Oddly, part of the explanation may rest in the seriousness of the consequences attached to grades and the fear that changing grading might disrupt the traditions that yield those consequences" (p. 3). There needs to be a deeper understanding and rationale for our grading practice if this work is to be meaningful.

Thomas Guskey and Jane Bailey (2010) suggest that teachers need to begin by clarifying the purpose of grading. They identified three key questions they believe educators must answer when defining the purpose for grades on a report card:

1.　What information will be communicated in the report card?
2.　Who is the primary audience for the information?
3.　What is the intended goal of the communication? [Or, How should the information be used?] (Guskey & Bailey, 2010, p. 32)

What changes might you need to work into your grading practice based on your responses to these questions? Knowing what to change might not be easy as a new teacher, but do consider what you could do initially that addresses some of the negative aspects of grading.

Tom Hierck and Garth Larson (2018) suggest four key considerations when determining your grading policy.

1. Homework and quizzes are viewed as formative practice in the learning progression and not counted toward a summative grade for academics.

2. Reassessment (retakes or redos) is allowed on all summative assessments.

3. Nonacademic factors (behaviors and life skills) are not counted in the summative academic grade, and students receive separate grades for behaviors or life skills.

4. Only student proficiency toward learning targets is used in reaching a summative conclusion on a student's academic grade.

Again, some of these might run counter to the policy at the school or district that hired you (and we're certainly not telling you to put your job at risk over this). However, you can minimize the impact of those things that might be misaligned with meaningful grading, in particular having nonacademic factors influencing the grades both negatively (penalty points often arbitrarily assigned) and positively (bonus points for bringing class supplies like tissues). When you encounter behavioral challenges, look to the strategies we provided in chapter 4 (page 45), but never punish students academically for a behavior issue.

We discuss the notion of second chances in the next section, as it is an entirely different area that confuses grading, often based on long-held fallacies about what happens after school. Ultimately the grade a student earns must be as clean and pristine in relationship to the learning outcomes (academic and behavioral) we expect they will master.

Offer Second Chances

Teachers and classrooms who incorporate effective grading practices understand that not all students become proficient at the same time or by following the same instruction. To paraphrase Richard DuFour and colleagues (2016), learning must be the constant, while the time to learn is the variable. Therefore, teachers should provide students with multiple opportunities to demonstrate they are proficient with lesson content and standards.

Rick Wormeli (2011) explains many teachers believe "they are building moral fiber and preparing students for the working world by denying them the opportunity to redo assignments and assessments" (p. 22). Not allowing retakes has the opposite effect. Wormeli (2011) further suggests, "the goal of education is that *all* students learn the content, not just the ones who can learn on the uniform timeline" (p. 22, italics added).

We often hear that second-chance opportunities don't exist in the "real world" or that teachers have to prepare students for a world where not everyone is successful. These colleagues ignore the myriad examples—doctors, pilots, lawyers, politicians, and teachers—all of whom have opportunities to take assessments to show proficiency in their profession multiple times without penalty. How many readers of this book failed their driver's test the first time? People make mistakes in their professions all the time, and most professions offer the opportunity to remedy those mistakes. We believe the same case should be made for students engaged in the learning process. Educators who incorporate effective grading and reporting practices believe it does not matter how long it takes to become proficient as long as students become proficient.

If a teacher identifies a learning outcome as need-to-know, how can it be that the student can opt out of the need? If it's essential, then every effort must be made to ensure all students "get it," even those who might need a second (or subsequent) chance to show what they know. Students should be graded according to their performance on specific goals (learning targets), not the routes they take to achieve those goals. Making students show new evidence of learning and reassessing until they meet their teacher's high expectations and goals demands more of students than letting them receive a failing grade and just moving on to whatever is next.

Allowing a second attempt at proficiency but limiting the results of that second attempt is a practice that should be long gone (for example, where the maximum achievement allowed is 70 percent or adding the second score to the first score, then dividing by two to get a new score). Yet these practices still exist. We must ask ourselves who benefits from this. Why should we penalize growth? Why set up another mathematical formulation to devalue the learning a student (and the teacher) have worked extra hard to produce?

You may recall taking swim lessons or may have enrolled your own children in lessons. Here's the requirements for the Red Cross (2014) Swim Kids Level 4: "Swimmers learn back swim and front crawl (10 m), work on flutter kick on back, perform kneeling dive, introduction to sculling, and can swim 25 meters continuously." Time is spent teaching these attributes, practicing them, and preparing for the demonstration of the skills. It doesn't matter where the swimmers were prior to the test day, nor does it matter how many times they have tried to demonstrate the skills. It just matters that they demonstrate the skills. Can you imagine the uproar if you were told that your current level (you can swim 25 meters) has to be added to your previous test level (you only made 15 meters, or you couldn't swim at all before some brilliant instruction), and you don't get your level completion certificate because the math doesn't add up to 25 meters?

When families and teachers bring up the concept of preparing their children for college or anything they are doing after high school, our response is the same: if we don't allow reassessment and only value first-time effort, we send them to college with gaps in their learning and additional struggles in their collegiate courses. We want students to realize the value of extra effort and be rewarded with gains in their competency and confidence.

Continuously remind students of the power of one of our most important three-letter words: y–e–t. When a student suggests they can't master the learning, complete the sentence for them by adding *yet*. Unfortunately, this can't happen if students' subsequent efforts are devalued and they determine the extra time is not worth the return.

With this belief firmly entrenched, it is equally important to establish a structured process, a procedure, that treats reassessment as an opportunity. Prior to any discussion about a reassessment opportunity, it must be clear that the initial effort by a student on the assessment represented their best effort in the moment. A student can't be ill-prepared for the initial assessment because they believe they are guaranteed a second chance. While we may agree that there is learning in failure, this can only occur if failure occurred as a result of something new emerging and not because of a lack of preparedness.

When you draft a reassessment procedure, consider the following items.

- Following their best first effort, students analyze their assessment and sort out items they were proficient at and those they had not yet mastered.

- For those items where proficiency has been attained, nothing further needs to occur. It is not necessary to check proficiency again with further assessment items.

- For those areas where proficiency was not attained, students will determine if the mistake was simple (students know what or how to do and just need practice) or complex (students do not know what or how to do and require more instruction).

- Students create a plan for additional instructional time (if needed and in collaboration with the teacher) and determine when the reassessment will occur (again, in collaboration with the teacher).

- Once proficiency is attained, the grade or information is shared. In other words, the grade that appears for reporting purposes is the grade the student has earned without averaging or setting an upper limit.

Figure 6.2 (page 78) is an example of a reassessment ticket.

Plan Interventions Driven by Evidence

Response to intervention (RTI) is a system in which every student receives the time and support they need to learn:

> RTI's underlying premise is that schools should not delay providing help for struggling students until they fall far enough behind to qualify for special education, but instead should provide timely, targeted, systematic interventions to all students who demonstrate the need. (Buffum, Mattos, & Weber, 2012, p. xiii)

Student Information
Name:
Grade:
Date:

Teacher Information
Name:
Subject:
Assignment or assessment:
Original score:
Desired score:

Reason for Reassessment
Please briefly explain why you are requesting a reassessment. Include any relevant information regarding any circumstances that justify this request.

Reassessment Details
Date:
Additional instructions:

Approval
I approve the request for a reassessment and confirm that the new due date is reasonable. I have provided any necessary instructions for the reassessment.
Teacher's signature:
Date:

Please fill in the Student Information section and hand it to your teacher. The teacher will complete the rest of the ticket. When you get it back, review it. Upon approval, you will be granted the opportunity to complete the reassessment by the specified due date.

Figure 6.2: Example reassessment ticket.

*Visit **go.SolutionTree.com/teacherefficacy** for a free reproducible version of this figure.*

Hierck and Weber (2023) suggest that RTI can inform future practice by examining the following questions.

- To what extent—and with what success—did the team guide all students toward mastery?

- What concepts or skills need to be reviewed with the entire class?

- What factors have contributed to student difficulties?

- What additional strategies and resources do the team need to ensure students improve their mastery?

- What patterns can the team identify from student errors?

- Among data team members, which instructional strategies proved most effective?

- Among data team members, which instructional strategies proved ineffective?
- How can the team improve the assessment?
- Which students need more time and an alternative approach?
- With which standards and skills do these students need more time and an alternative approach?

As you read through these questions, one essential fact about RTI has to be paramount—intervention is not a permanent state or label. When teachers intervene, it must be with an eye toward closing a gap, not simply acknowledging that gap or, even worse, growing the gap. RTI is not a precursor or gateway to special education. In reality, when performed well, RTI lessens the pressure on special education by clarifying what the gaps are and intervening to close those gaps. In fact, RTI at Work is very clear that students should never lose access to grade- or course-level instruction when learning missing skills, regardless of the level of intervention needed (Buffum, Mattos, & Malone, 2018).

While we recognize that each school year is unique, it must be stressed that the key to any RTI success resides in the core instruction provided to all students—what is often referred to as Tier 1 (Buffum et al., 2018). In other words, a higher number of students identified as Tier 2 (additional help for students who struggle to keep up with core instruction) or Tier 3 (intensive remediation for students who lack essential grade- or course-level skills) must be first tracked by evidence. What is occurring in the core Tier 1 instruction (Buffum et al., 2018)?

Tips to Thrive

When it comes to RTI, evidence is key. Beginning with the core instruction you provide (known as Tier 1), always be on the lookout for specific evidence that shows why a student might need a Tier 2 or Tier 3 intervention. Once you gather that evidence, it's a lot easier to figure out what a student needs.

The evidence gathered should inform what needs to happen and for how long (the intervention) in order to close the gaps in student learning. Tier 1 core instruction must be based on the students currently in your classroom—not last year's students or your best group of students. This ensures that the evidence gathered is timely and accurate and that the intervention is targeted and offers the best likelihood of ameliorating any deficits.

Final Thoughts: Mastery and Outcomes

This chapter examined a key challenge every teacher experiences: ascertaining that their students have mastered the desired learning outcomes. This is not an easy process and involves numerous key considerations, many of which this chapter identified.

Ultimately, every teacher must have confidence that the information they share with their students (and the adults in their students' lives) is accurate and related to the desired learning outcomes, both academically and behaviorally. Any elements that cloud the information shared will hinder the accuracy and impact the ability of the teacher to ensure that all students master those desired outcomes.

CHAPTER 7

How Do I Work With Parents and Guardians?

Every time a student enters our classroom, they bring with them a lifetime of experiences, opinions, and . . . *their family*. Students are an inevitable extension of their families, and their families are an extension of them. Some students come to school each day with a tremendous amount of support from their family, while others are seemingly left on their own to navigate the daily complexities of our education system. Our ability as teachers to work with their parents, guardians, and families is a critical component to helping our students (and ourselves) succeed:

> When [families] are engaged in their children's lives at school, students know they have the home support and knowledge they need to not only finish their work, but to apply that skill as they continue to develop a lifelong love of learning. (Eller & Hierck, 2021, p. 107)

When it comes to parents and guardians being involved in their child's schooling, there are a lot of different levels out there. Sometimes the parent or guardian that you need to speak with the most is the hardest to get hold of. Some parents you never need to contact because they're already emailing you about the grade their child got, the work they need to make up, or something that happened in class that day.

When a parent is hard to connect with, there's usually a pretty good reason for it, and it's rarely because they don't care about their child's education. You will have students whose parents and guardians risked their lives to leave their home country with the hope that their child would someday sit, in a new country, in a classroom like yours. Now they are working several jobs to build a life in the community where you teach. How can we compare that level of caring to the parent who has the time to constantly monitor every homework assignment and take the lead on the school fundraiser? (You can't.)

Regardless of how frequently you are able to interact with parents and guardians, or how often they show up to school events, keeping in mind how much families care and how they're doing the best they can with the information, knowledge, and skills they have, will be a tremendous help in your interactions (or lack of) with them.

Of course, there are some strategies you can use to connect and build relationships with all of your students' parents and guardians. Fortunately, this chapter is devoted to sharing the following important lessons we, along with many other teachers, have learned along the way about how we can make this all work to support the students in our classrooms.

- Remember that *parent*, *guardian*, and *family* can mean different things.
- Find parents' and guardians' preferred contact method.
- Use the power of questioning.
- Invite parents and guardians in.

Remember That *Parent*, *Guardian*, and *Family* Can Mean Different Things

If you haven't already, you will soon notice that we use the term *parents and guardians* throughout this chapter, and we always encourage teachers to use those words instead of just *parent*. That includes the many students whose families don't have two parents but rather a single parent, grandparents, foster parents, older siblings, other relatives, or even those who are unrelated. As you get to know your students, you'll come to realize that students have a lot of different living situations. Those situations will range from students who have seemingly everything (and even much more than they need) to students whose living situations will break your heart.

Always remember what every student in your class has in common: they have *you* as their teacher. You might not be able to control what happens outside of school, but your classroom can be the place where they are safe. Your school can be the place they know they are going to eat breakfast and lunch and be among friends. As the teacher, you can be the adult in their life that many students will look to for guidance and stability. Ensure that your classroom is welcoming and family friendly—whatever a student's particular family may look like. Consider these suggestions:

> [You should] post signs in multiple languages that are reflective of your population, and decorate your room and adjoining hallways with works of art and flags of countries represented in your community. Attend cultural events, as parents and community members enjoy seeing educators outside the school setting involved in the community. (Eller & Hierck, 2021, p. 116)

Find Parents' and Guardians' Preferred Method of Contact

Have you ever tried calling or texting someone you know and didn't get a reply? But then you reach out on social media and get a return message almost instantly? Very likely, it's not that they were intentionally ignoring your calls and texts, it just wasn't their preferred method of contact. Surveying your students' parents and guardians at the beginning of the year (when they are most accustomed to filling out surveys and forms) and finding out how they prefer to be contacted can give you a big advantage when you need to contact them throughout the year. Of course, it's always smart to have more than one method.

A quick online survey or form to fill out is all you need. Ask them to rank their top two methods of being contacted. Not only will this create some buy-in from the parents and guardians, it creates some accountability as well, all while giving them choice. Figure 7.1 offers a form from Alex's book *101 Tips for Teaching Online* that you can use for this purpose.

What is your preferred method of being contacted? (Write a 1 next to the box you most prefer and a 2 next to the box of your second preference.)

(Important note: Only provide contact methods that you are willing to do.)

☐ Text me. (Please provide cell phone number.) _____

☐ Call me. (Please provide phone number.) _____

☐ Email me. (Please provide email address.) _____

☐ Mail me a letter. (Please provide mailing address.)

_____

_____

_____

☐ Use social media. (Please provide preferred platform and username.)

_____   _____

Source: Kajitani, 2022, p. 72.

Figure 7.1: Sample contact preferences email.

*Visit **go.SolutionTree.com/teacherefficacy** for a free reproducible version of this figure.*

To save yourself some time (and frustration), it's a good idea to create a spreadsheet with parent and guardian contact information, along with the preferred method of contact that they indicated. Many online survey apps will automatically put all of the information into a spreadsheet for you, and you can access this spreadsheet when you need to reach out. Hopefully, you'll be able to get hold of them on the first (OK, maybe second) try.

Of course, it's important to be mindful about your approach to contacting them about the tough stuff and not forgetting to contact them about the good stuff. For many of us growing up, a phone call home from the teacher meant one thing: *we were in trouble*! For parents and guardians whose children are always getting into trouble, that's a lot of phone calls home. After a while, they probably don't want to answer the calls at all.

But what if you start the year by letting families know about something super positive that happened in class that day, like how their child treated one of their classmates with kindness? Or, what if you sent a quick text to let them know their child passed a mathematics test after struggling to add fractions with unlike denominators?

By reaching out to deliver positive news from time to time, you build trust, rapport, and a relationship with parents and guardians. Plus, a student is much less likely to act out in class or cause problems when they know you are in regular contact with their parents or guardians.

Here are ten positive reasons to reach out to parents and guardians.

1. You saw a student treat another student with a lot of respect.

2. You observed a student overcoming a struggle.

3. You took note of a good or improved grade on an assignment, quiz, or test. (Remember, *good* doesn't necessarily mean *high*; making progress is still worth celebrating.)

4. The student is always on time to class

5. You overheard a student say something really nice about their own family, and you want to share it with them. (Parents and guardians need good news about themselves as well.)

6. You had some sort of class competition, and the student did well (especially if they normally don't).

7. The student will receive an award or recognition at school.

8. You notice that the student has a unique talent (such as public speaking or something artistic), and you want to let the parents or guardians know so they can continue to encourage their child to continue developing it.

9. The student brightens up the class in their own unique way.

10. You just want to say "Thank you" for something that deserves acknowledgment.

Obviously, there are way more than just ten reasons. Keep an eye out for more positive reasons, and don't be afraid to reach out and let the parents and guardians know.

Use the Power of Questioning

Many parents and guardians want to support their child's education in any way they can; they often just don't know how. That's because they aren't teachers. They haven't studied effective teaching strategies, don't have teaching credentials, and haven't spent time in charge of a classroom. Despite this, they still want to help, and you can give them a place to start, and it's not as hard as you might think. It can even be very rewarding for teachers and families alike. And it starts with asking the right questions.

The following sections highlight the following four strategies: (1) questions you might give to parents and guardians, (2) questions you give to students, (3) ways to ask for advice from parents and guardians, and (4) the value of simply asking parents and guardians how they're doing.

Tips to Thrive

When reaching out to families, don't be afraid to use a translator. Not speaking the same language as the parent or guardian should not stop you from communicating with them. Many schools have someone who can help translate for you, and they can simply jump on a call with you and the parent or guardian or arrange for them to come to a scheduled meeting. For simple text communications, there are plenty of translation apps that can be very helpful as well. Google Translate (https://translate.google.com), DeepL (www.deepl.com/en/translator), Microsoft Translator (https://translator.microsoft.com), and Translate (www.translate.com) are apps that can provide great support to parents and guardians working to acquire a new language.

Using a translator not only helps everyone be clear in their communication, it also takes the pressure off parents and guardians to speak and understand English, which can be very intimidating for anyone who is not comfortable with the dominant language used in the school.

Give Parents and Guardians Some Questions They Can Ask Their Child

Have you ever had a conversation with your own child that goes something like this?

> **Parent or guardian:** How was school today?

> **Child:** It was OK.

> **Parent or guardian:** Did you do anything fun?

> **Child:** Not really.

What if, instead of subjecting the parents, guardians, and students to this conversation over and over again, we proactively gave parents and guardians three specific questions they could ask their children that might lead to further discussion? In an email, text, or on social media, you can send questions each day (or week, or whatever works best for you and your time). The key is to provide questions that families can ask without having been in class. Figure 7.2 (page 86) is an example of an email.

Subject: 3 Questions/3 Preguntas

Hi fourth-grade families. This week, we learned about three types of fractions. Here are three questions you can ask your child:

1) What is the difference between the numerator and the denominator?
2) What is an improper fraction?
3) Where do you see fractions in your life?

Hola familias de cuarto grado. Esta semana, aprendimos sobre tres tipos de fracciones. Aquí hay tres preguntas que puede hacerle a su hijo:

1) ¿Cuál es la diferencia entre el numerador y el denominador?
2) ¿Qué es una fracción impropia?
3) ¿Dónde ves las fracciones en tu vida?

Alex Kajitani
Teacher, Highland Elementary

Figure 7.2: Example email of questions that parents and guardians can ask students at home.

In the pictured email, there are two things to notice. First, the email is translated into Spanish. If you have parents or guardians who speak a language other than English, translating it into their language gives them instant access to the information. Second, notice that all three of the questions are specific to a lesson Alex just taught to his students, but the parents and guardians do not need to have been in the class to use them to engage their child in a conversation. By giving them the exact questions to ask, all they need to do is ask and, in many cases, learn from their child!

Give Students Some Questions They Can Ask at Home

Building on the previous idea of giving parents and guardians some questions they can ask, another easy idea is to give students questions *they* can ask at home. For example, after teaching an art lesson, simply say to your students, "Go home and ask your parents or guardians who two of their favorite artists are." For students who have families who aren't present at home after school, invite them to call, text, or otherwise message their parents or guardians. Then be sure to say, "Tomorrow, I'm going to ask you what they said."

Keep the questions simple and short (and age appropriate). Sometimes students will get brief, limited answers from their parents and guardians. Sometimes it will lead to a much longer conversation. Either way, you'll be getting the families involved in their child's education whether they realize it or not.

Here are a few examples of questions students could ask.

- After teaching a lesson on photosynthesis, have students ask their families, "Have you ever grown any plants or tried to grow your own food?"

- After teaching a lesson on World War II, have students ask their families, "Have you ever been in a combat zone or known someone who has been?"

- After an activity in physical education, have students ask their families, "What were your favorite outdoor games to play when you were my age?"

Again, keep the questions simple and short, and students will be much more likely to go home and ask them.

Ask Parents and Guardians for Advice

There will be times when you need to have a difficult conversation with a parent or guardian about something their child did (or didn't do) in class, or you might have to address a situation where emotions might be running high for everyone involved. Instead of diving right in on whatever the problem or challenge is, consider starting with the line, "I wanted to get your advice on something." Then explain the situation.

By starting out by saying you want their input, you remove any you-versus-them power dynamic that might be in play and create a sense that you're all in this together for the sake of their child. This focuses families on understanding the situation and helping the student (who is their child) succeed. At the same time, it shifts the responsibility from you needing to deal with the situation by yourself to having the parents or guardians take on some of the accountability for the solution.

Asking for advice is especially helpful when you need to tell families about a student whose behavior was challenging or about an incident that occurred in class. At the same time, it allows you to deliver the news in a matter-of-fact way that isn't blaming or shaming. And you might even get some great advice!

Here's an example of how this could work.

> **You:** Hi, Ms. Acosta. This is Mr. Chenowith, Julio's social science teacher at Garvey Middle School. Am I catching you at a good time?
>
> **Parent or guardian:** Yes, I have a few minutes.
>
> (Remember that the parent will probably be a bit tentative about why you're calling, so this simple prompt helps give them back a measure of control about talking with you.)
>
> **You:** I really enjoy having Julio in my class, and I wanted to get your advice on something.
>
> (You opened with something nice and are now creating that "we're all in this together" vibe.)
>
> **Parent or guardian:** Uh, OK . . . .

(It might not seem like much, but the parent or guardian is now invested in the situation, and you are free to tell them about it.)

You: Well, I'm having the challenge with Julio saying rude and disrespectful things to me and some of the other students. For example, earlier today, he was out of his seat and wandering around the classroom while the rest of the students were sitting and working. When I asked him to please sit down and start working on his assignment, he said, "Man, shut up and don't tell me what to do." Since you know Julio way better than I do, I wanted to get your advice on what to do in that situation, as I can't have the students talking to me this way.

(You've stated the situation and told the parent exactly what the student said; you've also reiterated that you're coming to them for advice.)

At this point, there is no point in scripting what the parent or guardians will say. They will say whatever they're going to say; however, keep the following things in mind as this conversation moves forward.

- **Don't continue the conversation if a parent or guardian berates you:** If the conversation goes in a way where you are feeling attacked or uncomfortable, it's OK to say, "Well, I need to end this conversation. Thank you for your time." You don't need to give an explanation as to why. You gave it your best shot, and you'll find a different way to deal with the situation.

- **There's often more than just the reason you're calling:** When a student is displaying challenging behavior in the classroom, as we discussed in chapter 4 (page 45), there is often a lot more than just that behavior happening behind the scenes. Often, parents and guardians will tell you about it. You can also just ask, "Is there anything happening at home that might help me better understand the situation?" The answers you get will range from heartbreaking to inspiring, and they'll always give you deeper insight into the situation.

- **Keep a record of what was discussed:** Immediately after the call, write down or record what you discussed during the conversation while it's fresh in your mind. This will be especially helpful if you ever need to have another conversation with that parent or guardian, or if anyone (such as an administrator) ever wants to know what was discussed. It's always easier and more accurate to pull out the notes you immediately took after a conversation than to try to recall it from memory.

- **Err on the side of caution and support:** You may have felt some hostility from a parent or guardian prior to a face-to-face meeting. You may be concerned about the student's well-being following a meeting. In situations like these, don't hesitate to reach out to your school administration for support in the meeting. It will go a long way to ensuring that the meeting stays on topic and emotions stay in check.

Ask Parents and Guardians How They're Doing

As teachers, we get overwhelmed and stressed out, and there are times when we just don't know what to do. The same is true for families. In the modern, ever-changing world, parenting can feel lonely, awkward, and much like teaching, with constant questioning of whether you're "doing it right." The impact of social media in their children's lives while they struggle to understand it can leave parents and guardians feeling further disconnected. Schools have changed considerably in a generation, and not knowing how or where to access support and information may lead to further isolation. Chances are, if their child is challenging at school, that child might also be challenging at home.

Taking a moment to genuinely ask a parent or guardian how *they* are doing isn't something that most parents and guardians are used to hearing from school or their children's teachers. It might even take them back momentarily—but it will always be appreciated. Some might give you a quick, shallow answer (and that's fine), while others might give you some insight into a part of their lives that you weren't expecting. Either way, they'll see how much you care. Building a relationship with the families all goes toward a better relationship with the student, so everyone wins.

Invite Parents and Guardians In

You have a wide variety of students and abilities in your classroom, so it only makes sense that you have a wide variety of parents and guardians as well. Some parents really want to know what is happening in class, but they don't want to be "assigned" any work. Using the words "I'd like to invite you to . . ." is a welcoming, nonthreatening way to provide parents and guardians with an opportunity to engage with and support their children. Just make sure there aren't any penalties for parents and guardians who aren't able to accept your invitation.

Here are a few things you can say to invite families to get involved. These work great in an email or as a post on your class social media page.

- "Today we watched a great video on [insert topic]. I invite you to watch it as well, and I'm sure your child will want to watch it again." [Insert link to the video.]

- "After reading an article on [insert topic], our class had a wonderful discussion. I invite you to read the article as well, and continue the conversation at home." [Attach the article or link to it.]

- "The students are engaged in an online game we've been playing that builds their skills in [insert topic]. I invite you to give it a shot as well and see how you do." [Insert a link to the game.]

- "This past week, we've been using the website [include website] as a resource for some of the activities we've been doing in class. I invite you to visit the site as well—it's packed with lots of great information."

If you're having a one-on-one conversation, try something like this: "I hear you work as [insert job], and I wanted to invite you to be a guest speaker in our classroom to tell the students about it. You could come in, or we could do it over Zoom."

Your invitations can also be a little more hands-on than the preceding recommendation. The following is a bit more of an advanced strategy, but it can be very effective. Remember, parents and guardians *want* to help their children, and may not know how. Most haven't taken classes (or read books like this one) on how to teach. By showing them some simple teaching strategies that they can use when helping their child at home, it can greatly increase the learning and empower families to feel like partners in their child's learning.

Here are two simple strategies that come from *101 Tips for Teaching Online* (Kajitani, 2022): (1) think time and (2) I do, we do, you do (often known as gradual release of responsibility). We encourage you to have families try them at home.

Think Time

You may observe parents and guardians asking their child a question and, when the child doesn't immediately answer, quickly answering for the child. The adults may not want to wait out the awkward silence that results while the child is thinking, or perhaps they think their child doesn't know the answer.

Take a moment to explain the importance of think time to parents and guardians, and teach them to silently count to ten before speaking again. It can even be a relief for the adults to know it's OK (and preferred) to relax and give their child time to consider the question, formulate an answer, and then express that answer—and that it's perfectly normal (for children and adults) to take a moment to formulate a thoughtful response to a question (McCarthy, 2018).

I Do, We Do, You Do

Whether it's a household chore, a mathematical procedure, or showing off those dance moves from high school, the *I do, we do, you do* strategy (Fisher & Frey, 2021) is a great way for parents and guardians to help show their child how to do something.

Figure 7.3 provides two examples of what this strategy might look like in action. The first example shows a child how to tie their shoelaces and the second provides simple reading instruction.

	Example: Tying Shoelaces	Example: Simple Reading Instruction
I Do	The adult sits next to the child, with their feet next to each other. The adult ties and unties their own shoelaces over and over again, explaining how they're doing it, perhaps even breaking it up into smaller steps. The child is simply watching, with no pressure to start doing it themselves.	The adult sits next to the child, with the book on the table between them. The adult reads a sentence (or more than one sentence, depending on the child's reading ability). The adult reads the sentence aloud, then pauses.
We Do	The child then starts trying it with their own shoes, but with the adult helping. The adult and child both have their hands on the laces, practicing over and over again, until the child starts showing that they can do it on their own.	The adult invites the child to read the sentences aloud with them (at the same time), and the adult adjusts their reading speed to keep pace with the child.
You Do	The adult starts to separate from the child, encouraging the child to do it on their own. The child might need a reminder or help on occasion, but for the most part, they can complete the task on their own.	The adult then invites the child to read the sentences aloud on their own, and then silently until the child feels confident.

Source: Kajitani, 2022, p. 67.

Figure 7.3: I do, we do, you do strategy example.

Remember, if you make your own videos explaining the preceding strategies, you can send them out whenever you need or post them on your class website so parents and guardians always have access to them. If you don't make your own videos, a quick internet search will help you easily find some that work.

Final Thoughts: Working Together

As a teacher, you will have a significant impact on your students' lives. They'll remember you, quote you, and use what they learned from you for many years to come. For many students, the only people who will have a larger impact on their lives are their parents and guardians. So let's do everything we can to work together. It's not easy, but when we make the effort to reach out to, connect with, and partner with families, we greatly increase our students' (and our own) chances for success. An added bonus is that teaching also becomes a lot more fun!

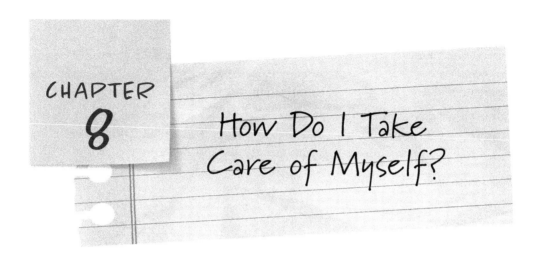

CHAPTER
8

How Do I Take
Care of Myself?

Educators are notorious for putting self-care low on their to-do list, but it is essential. You simply can't help others if you are not at your very best. There's a reason why flight attendants tell passengers to put their own oxygen masks on first in an emergency. They recognize that those who are in a position to help won't remain able to if they can't get enough oxygen. Think of *self-care* as *health care*. It's what every teacher needs so they can be at their very best and offer support to the students they serve each day.

Look at the graphic in table 8.1 and make a note of any that you have experienced (or still are experiencing).

Table 8.1: Stress Responses

Mind	Emotions	Body	Behavior
• Concentration trouble • Memory trouble • Decision-making trouble • Dread • Negative self-perception • Dissociation (feeling unreal)	• Overwhelmed • Restless • Sad • Hopeless • Anxious • Irritable	• High heart rate • Tense muscles • Headache • Stomach ache • Fatigue • High blood pressure	• Difficulty sleeping • Always or never being alone • Less motivation for physical movement • Heightened startle response • Crying more than normal • Eating more or less than normal

Source: Adapted from DeWolfe, 2000; Luster, 2021.

Did you check something off in each quadrant? Perhaps even more than one? We don't offer this to create panic but instead to create awareness. Everyone experiences some combination of these stress responses at some point, and we have strong reasons to believe that a moderate baseline of short-term stress can be good for you (Sanders, 2013). However, when these responses become chronic and impact your overall quality of life, these entirely acceptable and very human responses serve to undermine your best efforts. More importantly, left unchecked, they will make it virtually impossible for you to be your best self. That best self is more than enough for your students and colleagues, and you need to be firing on all cylinders to be that person.

In this chapter, we explore the following ways you can ensure self-care becomes a greater priority in your life while also clarifying that self-care is not selfish! It's essential for you to do the incredible things you do every day in your classroom.

- Understand your self-care options.
- Take time for yourself.
- Foster relationships and connectedness.
- Manage your secondary traumatic stress.
- Recognize and control your emotions.

Understand Your Self-Care Options

Self-care is really about focusing on your physical, mental, and emotional health so that you're prepared to be the best teacher you can be for yourself, your students, and your community. It's also very personal in the sense that it's about any action you may take to improve your health and well-being. In other words, it won't look the same for everybody.

Tom loves to run, while Alex enjoys surfing. Both of them try to engage in these activities as frequently as they can each week, but neither is very keen to adopt the routines of the other. According to the National Alliance on Mental Illness (n.d.), self-care includes six elements, for which they provide an online self-care inventory (bit.ly/3Y9oZUk) that you can take.

1. **Physical:** This encompasses all of your physiological needs that contribute to you being at your physical best to take on the role of being a teacher. Are you eating properly, getting enough sleep, exercising, and taking care of yourself?

2. **Psychological:** How are your mental health and well-being as you address your needs for self-reflection, gratitude, growth opportunities, and coping with stress?

3. **Emotional:** While teachers are often great at looking after their students' emotional needs, they sometimes forget their own needs in this domain. Grace for self is key here. Spending time with people you value and who value you can be very reaffirming.

4. **Spiritual:** While this may lead you to practice your faith, it is not meant to only include organized spirituality. Time for reflection, spending time in nature, or contributing to your community can all be rejuvenating.

5. **Social:** We are all part of a larger circle. Interacting with others, including those outside your profession, can be a breath of fresh air and allow you to unplug from the challenges that accompany being a teacher.

6. **Professional:** Connections to your peers can be invigorating. Be fascinated by the adult talent that comes to work every day in your school. Learn from those who are least like you but achieving great results. Continue being a learner who is curious.

As you contemplate your own healthy self-care plan, aim for an activity that might fall under each of these elements. These activities can be as small as drinking water every day to taking up a new activity like yoga.

A challenge with self-care is that it occasionally gets misrepresented as self-indulgence. Christine Meinecke (2010) clarifies this when she suggests, "Self-indulgence is characterized by avoidance of the effortful and substitution of quick and easy antidotes." However, the behaviors chosen are generally temporary stress relievers, such as alcohol or junk food consumption or binge-watching television. While these behaviors may provide quick relief, they also have detrimental long-term health effects. Self-care implies a positive focus aimed at managing and preventing stress and exhaustion while promoting benefits to your overall well-being.

Periodically we hear from colleagues about the seemingly impossible challenge of finding time to effectively practice self-care. While it's unlikely that you have many moments in a day that are not filled with something else, ideally, you can include a couple of self-care practices throughout the day. Make it a priority to close your eyes and breathe mindfully for two minutes at lunch, before your student arrives for extra help, and get out of your chair and stretch for two minutes during your plan time or between classes (MindPeace, 2020). Modeling self-care also demonstrates to students the importance of establishing this habit for themselves. The remainder of this chapter offers a collection of more specific strategies that you can put to good use for your long-term well-being.

Take Time For Yourself

Educator wellness expert and best-selling author Tina H. Boogren is a colleague of ours and, by her own admission, a "fierce advocate for educators, particularly for their well-being" (Solution Tree, n.d.). A prolific speaker, she's authored and coauthored numerous books on self-care for educators, among them *Educator Wellness* (Kanold & Boogren, 2022) and its complement, *The Educator Wellness Plan Book and Journal* (Boogren, Kanold, & Kullar, 2024), which is loaded with tools for planning and engaging in self-care. Her mission is ensuring that teachers focus on their own wellness so that they can support student wellness. It's not an either/or proposition but a focus on the power of *and*, which is to say, educators can be effective in the classroom while also tending to their needs.

She poses some great questions that are worth reflecting on (Boogren, 2018, p. 4; italics in original).

- "What if teachers learn to take care of themselves *while* taking care of their students?"

- "What if you split your time between your own and students' needs in a new way?"
- "What if, for every move you make for the sake of your students, you also make a move for your own sake?"
- "What if you not only engaged in professional development on pedagogy and content, but also spent time learning how to best support yourself?"

Boogren builds the essential case around reminding teachers that if you are drained and at wit's end by the end of each day, it's unlikely that you can support your students' needs. It's just not sustainable. However, as Boogren (2018) points out, "This is what we are asking educators to do, day in and day out. So many are struggling to stay afloat, without the tools to learn how to properly thrive" (p. 4). The good news is that she provides the tools to help teachers reimagine what can occur, and she makes the steps so tangible that it's almost impossible to not begin the journey to your own wellness. For example, the survey featured in figure 8.1 empowers you to gauge how often you engage in common and effective self-care practices. Please remember that the point of this survey is not to beat yourself up over what you're not doing but to create awareness about what you are already doing to engage in self-care and acknowledge what more you could do that will benefit your well-being.

Recognizing where you are and identifying growth opportunities are the best strategies to initiate change. Avoid labeling things as "weaknesses," and instead focus on the growth opportunity that lies before you. Your current baseline is the data you'll begin with, and then set some reasonable goals. For example, if you look at the first item and identify that you never drink six glasses of water every day, don't immediately go for six glasses a day. Instead, set a goal that is attainable for *you*. Start by making sure you drink just one or two glasses of water each day, and when you consistently maintain that goal, increase it. (And don't forget to celebrate your accomplishment!) Other goals in this survey can be more complicated to achieve, but you can achieve them, and the guidance in this chapter can help.

Foster Relationships and Connectedness

As we continue our work with colleagues, we see a striking similarity in what teachers share with us about the emotional load they bear. The most frequent shares we get coalesce around two themes: (1) affirmation and (2) anxiety. This mirrors the findings of the Yale/CASEL survey conducted in 2020, which had over 5,000 educators respond in just three days (Cipriano & Brackett, 2020). The educators described, in their own words, the feelings they had each day; the five most cited were (1) anxiety, (2) fear, (3) worry, (4) overwhelm, and (5) sadness (Cipriano & Brackett, 2020). By any assessment, these are chronic and serious forms of stress.

In the past week, how many days did you do the following?	Never (zero days)	Rarely (one day)	Sometimes (two to three days)	Often (four to five days)	Always (six to seven days)
Physiology					
I drank at least six glasses of water.					
I got at least seven hours of sleep.					
I ate a variety of nutritious foods from a range of food groups.					
I engaged in physical activity.					
Safety					
I felt safe at school.					
I felt safe at home or away from school.					
I felt a sense of order or consistency at school.					
I felt a sense of order or consistency at home or away from school.					
Belonging					
I felt included and respected at school.					
I felt included and respected at home or away from school.					
I felt like a coworker truly cared about my well-being.					
I felt like a family member or friend truly cared about my well-being.					

Figure 8.1: Self-care survey: Starting point.   Continued ▶

Esteem					
I spoke kindly to myself.					
I felt competent in my job.					
I felt important at home or school.					
Someone recognized the work I do at school or elsewhere.					
Self-Actualization					
I set personal goals at home or school.					
I believed I could accomplish what I set out to do.					
I had a positive outlook on the future at home or school.					
I had a moment of flow or a peak experience (where I felt totally, completely happy and at peace) at home or school.					
Transcendence					
I felt inspired at home or at school.					
I did something at home or at school for someone else without anyone asking me to.					
I felt empathy toward someone else or I forgave someone at home or at school.					
I felt a sense of gratitude or engaged in mindfulness.					

Source: Boogren, 2018, pp. 11–12.

*Visit **go.SolutionTree.com/teacherefficacy** for a free reproducible version of this figure.*

When individuals are left to resolve chronic stressors, the potential for burnout increases. Monique Valcour (2016) reminds us that the "best antidote to burnout is seeking out rich interpersonal interactions and continual personal and professional development." It's essential that you work together with your colleagues. Remember that, as "part of the collaborative team, you're either getting better at your job or helping someone else get better" (Williams & Hierck, 2015, p. 53).

The notion of affirmation falls in the domain of school leadership. One of the key relationships for those new to the profession (and critical as teachers continue their work) is the connection to one's principal. As one teacher commented in a *Business Insider* survey when asked what she wished she had known before starting her career, "Your happiness and success as a teacher depends to a certain extent on your principal" (Gillett, 2016). Supporting new teachers and helping them manage both the expected and the unexpected go a long way toward ensuring they feel supported and capable.

Even if you aren't in a position to have a structured team to tap into, you still have colleagues facing the same in-school challenges you do. It's important that you keep talking, and in the absence of a schoolwide collaborative effort, like a PLC, strive to have and maintain a buddy system on staff. Having routine check-ins with colleagues (and committing to checking in regularly) gives you people to lean on and share the load with. Eller and Hierck (2021) suggest this means "having an open environment where everyone is willing to help everyone, and where educators know that they can talk to other colleagues throughout the school" (p. 129). Creating an intentional buddy system among staff doesn't have to be complicated, either. Anything that establishes regular connections will move the needle: lunches, happy hours, quick talks between classes, or short meetings after school. These may be opportunities to reflect on the day, share successes, let go of the failures, or just keep a balance as you adjust to your school's rhythm.

Self-care requires that the adults in the building are supported and cared for, and you must be an advocate for you! Work with your colleagues to create an environment that is both a brave and safe space for yourself and for them. Finally, if your own mental health and wellness are declining, seek mental health support services for yourself. It's not a sign of weakness nor a reflection of your inability to cope.

Manage Your Secondary Traumatic Stress

The stress you experience as a teacher doesn't just come from your first-hand, lived experiences. It's not just the pressure of a grading deadline or the frustration of not being able to get through to a student. Teachers are also prone to absorbing the stress their students experience. Any teacher "who works directly with traumatized children and adolescents is vulnerable to the effects of trauma—referred to as *secondary traumatic stress*—being physically, mentally, or emotionally worn out, or feeling overwhelmed by students' traumas" (David, 2016, p. 79). Teachers should be aware of the "presence of post-traumatic stress disorder (PTSD) symptoms caused by at least one indirect exposure to traumatic material" (National Child Traumatic Stress Network, 2011, p. 2). The following sections explain symptoms of secondary traumatic stress and secondary (vicarious) transformation.

Symptoms of STS

The symptoms of secondary traumatic stress (STS) can mimic those of students who have experienced trauma. It can impact cognitive functioning, including attention and concentration. It can also affect emotional functioning. For example, teachers might experience increased irritability or agitation with students or feel numb or detached from their students' experiences, both good and bad (Kenardy, De Young, Le Brocque, & March, 2011).

Often, the best way to deal with this is through early recognition of the signs. Table 8.2 collects a series of signs of STS. It is intended to be informative and not create any undue concern if something on the list resonates with you.

Table 8.2: Signs of Secondary Traumatic Stress

Physical: • Sleeplessness • Chronic exhaustion	Behavioral: • Self-destructive behaviors • Changing routines, avoiding situations • Withdrawing
Occupational: • Problems planning classroom activities and lessons • Inability to listen, avoidance of responsibilities	Psychological: • Decreased concentration and attention • Increased agitation with students • Intense feelings, intrusive thoughts, or dreams about a student's trauma
Spiritual: • Questioning meaning of life • Lacking self-satisfaction	

Source: Adapted from Administration for Children and Families, n.d.

Tips to Thrive

Don't be afraid to ask for help. It's hard to give your best when you're not at your best, so if you are experiencing chronic secondary traumatic stress, don't hesitate to seek out professional support. As teachers, we tell our students never to be afraid to ask for help—and that goes for us as well!

There is occasionally some lack of clarity about PTSD, STS, and burnout. While some of the signs and symptoms may overlap, it's worth understanding the difference.

•   *Burnout* "is characterized by emotional exhaustion and a reduced feeling of personal accomplishment"(National Child Traumatic Stress Network, 2011, p. 2).

It is an accumulation of work-related stress and not a reflection of STS. Burnout might occur regarding a teacher trying to plan awesome lessons, meet standardized tests goals, and grade all of their students' tests in a timely manner. It can begin gradually and get progressively worse, but it is not related specifically to indirect trauma effects.

- *STS* happens after someone is indirectly exposed to threatening events, including hearing stories about students' trauma (Marsac & Ragsdale, 2020).
- *PTSD* happens when someone feels directly threatened (Marsac & Ragsdale, 2020).

As a teacher, you will have students who share some challenging moments and experiences with you, and these might impact you. Notwithstanding the reporting protocols you should be aware of in your school as they relate to any disclosure, make sure you receive the necessary support to manage your own mental health.

Charles Figley, the traumatologist who developed the concept of compassion fatigue, offers the following suggestions when examining secondary traumatic stress:

- **Be aware of the signs.** Educators with compassion fatigue may exhibit some [specific] signs.
- **Don't go it alone.** Anyone who knows about stories of trauma needs to guard against isolation.
- **[Recognize STS] as an occupational hazard.** When an educator approaches students with an open heart and a listening ear, STS can develop.
- **Seek help with your own traumas.** Any adult helping children with trauma, who also has his or her own unresolved traumatic experiences, is more at risk for compassion fatigue.
- **If you see signs in yourself, talk to a professional.** If you are experiencing signs of compassion fatigue for more than two to three weeks, seek counseling with a professional who is knowledgeable about trauma.
- **Attend to self-care.** Guard against your work becoming the only activity that defines who you are. (Figley, 1995, as cited in National Child Traumatic Stress Network, 2008, p. 1)

These factors mirror many of the sections covered in this chapter and are a reminder that self-care is a critical component in the work teachers do. Healthy eating, exercise, enjoyable activities away from work, and engaging in rest (not just sleep)—in other words, self-care—are all things that can help make you more resilient to STS.

Secondary (Vicarious) Transformation

A transformative outcome for teachers who are exposed to their students' challenges (and by extension their families') is equally impactful. You may witness, through your students, some of the more difficult aspects of life that people have experienced. This has the potential to alter your perspective and inform you in unanticipated ways. Being positively impacted and inspired by others' hurdles, and admiring their strength and perseverance, is *secondary transformation* (Safe Schools New Orleans, n.d.). It's important to reflect on these experiences and try to grow from them.

Many positive attributes can emerge as a result of this transformation, including those identified by researchers and mentioned here (Barrington & Shakespeare-Finch, 2013; Gibbons, Murphy, & Joseph, 2011; Splevins, Cohen, Murray, Bowley, & Joseph, 2010, as cited in Queensland Program of Assistance to Survivors of Torture and Trauma, 2016, p. 15):

- Deeper understanding of the world, suffering, and humanity's capacity to overcome adversity
- Greater sense of meaning
- Renewed, enriched and/or changed spirituality
- Greater value and appreciation of relationships
- Greater degree of compassion
- Greater understanding of various cultures
- Greater sense of fulfillment, purpose or pleasure

Remember that this potential for transformation occurs as a result of some intentionality on your part to work through and process the experiences you are having. There are many amazing stories of individuals (including some of you) who have overcome enormous obstacles to get where they are today. These can inspire teachers and help them overcome some of the challenges they face.

Recognize and Control Your Emotions

Being able to identify and control emotions can help you be successful. It is a challenge to remain calm when a student is having an emotional outburst and wants to draw you into that struggle. A student may push every button you have—and even discover one you did not know existed—and it's critical that *you* remain grounded in your principles. For example, if you believe that respect is a core value in your classroom, you'll need to model it when a student is being disrespectful. You will never teach a child about respect by out-disrespecting them.

To be clear, this is not about accepting and tolerating negative behavior; it is about processing such behavior in a respectful fashion. To do otherwise sends an overt message to students that it's more about power and control than modeling respect.

Figure 8.2 provides a place for you to record the emotions that you experience and gives you the opportunity to reflect on those emotions. The process requires you to list any emotions that you sometimes encounter during the day and asks you to reflect and strategize on them.

Emotion	How You Recognize This Emotion	Strategies You Use to Manage This Emotion

Source: © John Eller, 2022. Used with permission.

Figure 8.2: Recognize and control your emotions.

*Visit **go.SolutionTree.com/teacherefficacy** for a free reproducible version of this figure.*

Having the opportunity to reflect on the emotions and their potential causes allows you to plan and be proactive around those situations or individuals that may be prompting the emotions. This is not to suggest we advocate for avoiding those situations or individuals, as that is often impossible in your role as a teacher. Rather, it is to suggest that you formulate a plan using some of the strategies outlined in this book as a way forward.

Part of managing your emotions and reactions to stressors also includes recognizing what is within your control to influence at all. John and Sheila Eller (2009) do a lot of work with educators on school culture, and one piece of their work looks at clarifying the things that impact you over which you have control versus where your control is limited. As you think about the limited additional time and energy you have, where does it make the most sense to expend those resources? Where does it make sense to learn to let go?

Simply put, if you cannot control it, try not to get stressed about it. If you cannot influence it, try not to get upset about it. Focus on what you can change, not on what you cannot. To identify issues that you worry about and determine your level of control over them, follow these steps (adapted from Covey, 2004).

1. Draw one large circle and another, smaller circle inside it. The larger outer circle is the circle of concern. The smaller inner circle is the circle of control.

2. List three or four issues that you deal with on a regular basis.

3. Place them in the circles based on your level of control over these items.

4. Reflect on the following questions after you have identified items in each of the circles.

   ‣ What did you notice about the issues that you can *control* compared to those that *concern* you?

‣ How could you either reduce the number of issues you are concerned about or increase your scope of control over issues to help make you more comfortable?

‣ What do you plan to do as a result of completing this activity?

Final Thoughts: Plan Your Self-Care

This chapter focused on self-care and what results when we don't make it a priority. As you think about the content you've just read, connect your next steps to the actions in figure 8.3 and think about any changes you'd consider making. Remember, the point is to advocate *for yourself*, not compare yourself to anyone else or worry about what is missing. The last thing you need is for self-care to become another stressor in your life. Start with manageable plans and frame them with the stop, continue, and start framework.

• **Stop:** What are some practices that are not working that you'd like to stop?

• **Continue:** What are some practices that are going well that you'd like to continue or expand?

• **Start:** What are some practices, routines, or traditions you might like to start in your class?

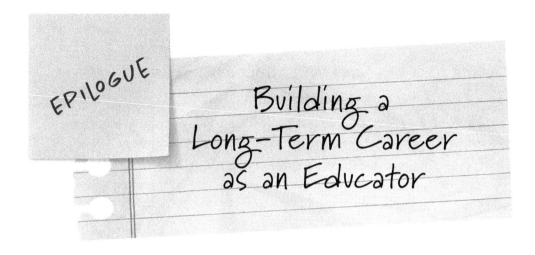

EPILOGUE

Building a Long-Term Career as an Educator

For many teachers, teaching is a job. It pays the bills—or at least it should—the hours are long but predictable, and although "summers off" is a term noneducators use when they describe our profession, it is a job that gives us time throughout the year to balance, rebalance, and enjoy our lives. It's a job that is filled with highs and lows, and it's an opportunity to spend time with students and alongside other teachers.

Equally, and often more prevalent, for many teachers, teaching isn't just something we do—teaching is what we are. Over the years, we interact with, guide, and build relationships with hundreds, even thousands, of students who leave a mark on our soul. We become known throughout the communities we teach in, and we laugh, cry, celebrate, and mourn alongside the people in our community because they are our students, they were our students, and over time, they may even be the children of our students.

Building a long-term career as an educator takes time and quite a bit of resilience, but when done with intention and thoughtfulness, the result can be a career that is fulfilling and rewarding in the knowledge that you're making an important impact in the world. Eric Richter, Rebecca Lazarides, and Dirk Richter (2021) identify four common motives for becoming a teacher—(1) career aspirations, (2) social contribution, (3) escaping routines, and (4) coincidence—with career aspirations tending to be the most significant aspect. We believe individuals become teachers to be difference makers—not chroniclers of what is, but partners in creating what could be.

Use these final sections of this book to inform your next steps and plan for a prosperous and rewarding future. You build a long-term career as an educator by doing the following.

- Define (or redefine) what success looks like.
- Deal with the money part of teaching.
- Build your network.
- Surround yourself with good people.
- Invest in yourself and your professional learning.
- Be reflective.

Define (or Redefine) What Success Looks Like

As educators, we're on a different career trajectory than most noneducators. Our success isn't marked by the money we make, the titles we obtain, or the next big promotion. We analyze test scores and IEPs rather than stock charts and profits and losses.

Ask yourself what career success means to *you*. Although your answer might change over time, knowing what success looks like, and having a deep understanding of what you value most, help keep things in perspective over the years, and can help keep you grounded when things get tough.

Deal With the Money Part of Teaching

We've all heard that teachers aren't "in it for the money," but for many young teachers, educating is a solid gig. They make enough to pay the bills, their health insurance is (mostly) covered, and the work, although tough, is fun and meaningful.

Five to ten years later, things can look much different. Those young teachers might now have a family that they need to provide for, as well as a mortgage and other bills. That same health insurance plan might not cover everyone else in the family. At this point, some teachers leave teaching and pursue work in another field. Others get a second job or take on additional paid responsibilities that they work on evenings, weekends, or during holidays. Others have spouses or partners who also work.

How you choose to manage your money is entirely up to you, and this section isn't going to give you financial planning or investment advice. Whether you're a young teacher or someone who has entered teaching later in life, it's important to plan ahead.

Build Your Network

Even though it might feel like you teach by yourself in your own classroom a lot of the time, teaching is a profession where you have the opportunity to meet a lot of people. Of course, you work with colleagues each day, and you'll meet other teachers throughout your district and attend conferences and events where you'll meet teachers from across the country and around the world. If you're ever at a loss for something to say, start with this: "Hi! I'm [name]. What do you teach?" You'll soon find yourself engaged in some meaningful dialogue with your new friend or colleague.

Building a solid network is critical to your success over the long term. There might be times (especially in your first few years) where your school undergoes budget and staffing cuts, and you will need to look elsewhere for a job. Knowing other teachers at other school sites can help keep you informed of which schools might have an opening that you can pursue.

There will also be times throughout your career where you need to tap into your network to get help with something—from getting questions answered, to raising money for a cause you and your students are pursuing. The wider and deeper your network, the more effectively you can get things done!

Surround Yourself With Good People

Surrounding yourself with good people is one of the best decisions you can make throughout your career, as you will inevitably take on the attitudes and attributes of those you hang out with most (Morin, 2015). In many teachers' lounges, there is a small group of teachers who eat lunch together and spend much of their time complaining about students. Go sit at that table, and you'll soon find yourself complaining about students.

There is also a group of teachers who love teaching, are continually trying to improve, and take a genuine interest in the colleagues they surround themselves with. Sit at that table, and you'll soon find yourself as one of them.

According to Adam Grant (2013), in his book *Give and Take: Why Helping Others Drives Our Success*, "Three decades of research show that receiving support from colleagues is a robust antidote to burnout. Having a support network of teachers is huge" (p. 177). So whenever and however possible, surround yourself with good people. People who care about you. People who help fill your soul. People who have your back. Also remember, they're choosing to sit with you as well.

Invest in Yourself and Your Professional Learning

As an educator, you'll have many opportunities throughout the years to participate in professional development where you'll learn about new ideas, strategies, and research that you can use to be more effective. The professional development you experience will range from inspiring and life changing to jaw-clenchingly boring; the venues can range from big conferences at fancy hotels and convention centers, to sitting alongside your colleagues in the teachers' lounge, discussing a teaching strategy that seems to be working. Regardless of the venue or topic, consider the following, which will help you make the most out of any professional development opportunities.

- Figure out how you learn best, and pursue those opportunities.
- Go in with questions you want answered.
- Leave with something you can implement.

Tips to Thrive

Remember that some PD days are going to be better than others.

Figure Out How You Learn Best, and Pursue Those Opportunities

Do you prefer a big conference filled with hundreds or thousands of educators from across the country, listening to big-name speakers who deliver well-crafted presentations? Or perhaps you prefer smaller meeting-style discussions, where you get to actively share and learn from the others in the room? In person or virtual? Notepad and pen to take notes or type directly into your device? Once you figure out the conditions you learn best in, pursuing those opportunities will not only help you learn and grow, it will greatly increase your chances of having fun!

Go In With Questions You Want Answered

As you prepare to attend the professional development opportunity, find out as much as you can about what it will focus on. Check in with yourself about what you already know about the topic. Then, formulate a few questions that you hope will be answered by the end. Looking for answers will give the time you're investing more meaning, help you stay focused throughout, and keep you open to new ideas.

Leave With Something You Can Implement

Not every professional learning opportunity is going to change the way you teach or think. But hopefully, each one will have *something*—even if it's small—that you can use to be more effective in the job you do. Try to identify that before it ends. As teachers, we are often so busy with the minute-to-minute act of teaching that it can be hard to implement a new idea that we learned a few days ago. Before you leave, identifying at least one thing that you can implement immediately, and then implementing it immediately, will ensure that your time and energy were well spent, and that you continue to develop as an educator.

Be Reflective

As a teacher, there will be times when things don't go well. There will be times when people give you advice, or suggestions on how you can improve. You'll even get criticized by your students or their parents or guardians. Whenever this happens, you have a choice: be reflective or get defensive.

Being reflective takes courage. When an administrator observes your teaching, and then makes some suggestions, it takes courage to not get defensive, and instead, consider the suggestions you received and how you might implement them.

When you have a bad day of teaching (and you'll have plenty of them), it takes courage to reflect on everything that happened that day, and instead of blaming the students, analyze deeply and honestly where you could have done a better job, and what you'll do differently tomorrow. When a student complains about something you did or said to their parent or guardian, and that adult is now complaining to you, it takes courage to listen respectfully, hear them out, and work toward a resolution. Any time you have a chance to be reflective instead of defensive, you will learn, grow, and evolve as an educator.

When We Teach, We Live Forever

Beauty fades, money runs out, and machines fall apart. Our ideas are the only true possessions that we can pass from one generation to the next. By defining (or redefining) what our own true definition of success is and figuring out how we can manage on a teacher's salary, we put ourselves on the right path.

By building a network, surrounding ourselves with good people, and investing in our own professional development whenever possible, we ensure that that path continues to help us grow, evolve, and thrive. Building a long-term career as an educator means that you'll have endless opportunities to share your ideas, reflect on the work you do, and truly live forever.

REFERENCES AND RESOURCES

Administration for Children and Families. (n.d.). *Secondary traumatic stress.* Accessed at www.acf.hhs.gov/trauma-toolkit/secondary-traumatic-stress on October 1, 2023.

Advaney, M. (2017, May 6). *To talk or not to talk that is the question!* Accessed at https://youthtimemag.com/to-talk-or-not-to-talk-that-is-the-question-at-least-70-percent-of-communication-is-non-verbal on February 22, 2023.

ALICE. (n.d.). *7 tips for classroom setup to guard against a school shooter.* Accessed at www.alicetraining.com/alice-institute-training/7-tips-setting-classroom-support-alice-concepts on September 5, 2023.

Alter, P., & Haydon, T. (2017). Characteristics of effective classroom rules: A review of the literature. *Teacher Education and Special Education, 40*(2), 114–127.

Ambrose, S. A., Bridges, M. W., Lovett, M. C., DiPietro, M., & Norman, M. K. (2010). *How learning works: Seven research-based principles for smart teaching.* San Francisco: Jossey-Bass.

Arlinghaus, K. R., & Johnston, C. A. (2019). The importance of creating habits and routine. *American Journal of Lifestyle Medicine, 13*(2), 142–144. https://doi.org/10.1177/1559827618818044

Bailey, K., & Jakicic, C. (2023). *Common formative assessment: A toolkit for Professional Learning Communities at Work* (2nd ed). Bloomington, IN: Solution Tree Press.

Barrington, A. J., & Shakespeare-Finch, J. (2013). Working with refugee survivors of torture and trauma: An opportunity for vicarious post-traumatic growth. *Counselling Psychology Quarterly, 26*(1), 89–105. https://doi.org/10.1080/09515070.2012.727553

Black, P., & Wiliam, D. (1998). *Inside the black box: Raising standards through classroom assessment.* Accessed at https://kappanonline.org/inside-the-black-box-raising-standards-through-classroom-assessment on July 6, 2023.

Black, P., & Wiliam, D. (2009). Developing the theory of formative assessment. *Educational Assessment, Evaluation and Accountability, 21*(1), 5–31.

Boogren, T. H. (2018). *Take time for you: Self-care action plans for educators.* Bloomington, IN: Solution Tree Press.

Boogren, T. H., Kanold, T. D., & Kullar, J. K. (2024). *The educator wellness plan book and journal: Continuous growth for each season of your professional life.* Bloomington, IN: Solution Tree Press.

Botsman, R. (2017). *Who can you trust? How technology brought us together and why it might drive us apart.* New York: Public Affairs.

Brier, J., & Lanktree, C. B. (2013). *Integrative treatment of complex trauma for adolescents (ITCT-A) treatment guide* (2nd ed.). University of Southern California Adolescent Trauma Training Center. Accessed at https://keck.usc.edu/adolescent-trauma-training-center/wp-content/uploads/sites/169/2016/06/ITCT-A-TreatmentGuide-2ndEdition-rev20131106.pdf on July 6, 2023.

Brown, B. (2015). *Daring greatly: How the courage to be vulnerable transforms the way we live, love, parent, and lead.* New York: Avery.

Buffum, A., Mattos, M., & Malone, J. (2018). *Taking action: A handbook for RTI at Work.* Bloomington, IN: Solution Tree Press.

Buffum, A., Mattos, M., & Weber, C. (2012). *Simplifying response to intervention: Four essential guiding principles.* Bloomington, IN: Solution Tree Press.

California Department of Education. (2013). *California Common Core State Standards: English language arts & literacy in history/social studies, science, and technical subjects.* Sacramento: Author. Accessed at www.cde.ca.gov/be/st/ss/documents/finalelaccssstandards.pdf on June 16, 2023.

Carretié, L., Mercado, F., Tapia, M., & Hinojosa, J. A. (2001). Emotion, attention, and the "negativity bias," studied through event-related potentials. *International Journal of Psychophysiology, 41*(1), 75–85.

Cheryan, S., Ziegler, S. A., Plaut, V. C., & Meltzoff, A. N. (2014). Designing classrooms to maximize student achievement [Abstract]. *Policy Insights From the Behavioral and Brain Sciences, 1*(1), 4–12. https://doi.org/10.1177/2372732214548677

Cipriano, C., & Brackett, M. (2020, April 30). *How to support teachers' emotional needs right now.* Accessed at https://greatergood.berkeley.edu/article/item/ how_to_support_teachers _emotional_needs_right_now on February 8, 2023.

Clear, J. (n.d.). *How long does it actually take to form a new habit? (Backed by science).* Accessed at https://jamesclear.com/new-habit#:~:text=Interestingly%2C%20the%20researchers%20also%20found,all%2Dor%2Dnothing%20process. on July 6, 2023.

Collier-Meek, M. A., Sanetti, L. M. H., & Boyle, A. M. (2019). Barriers to implementing classroom management and behavior support plans: An exploratory investigation. *Psychology in the Schools, 56*(1), 5–17.

Comer, J. (1995). *Untitled presentation. Education Service Center, Region IV.* Houston, TX.

Cook, C. R., Fiat, A., Larson, M., Daikos, C., Slemrod, T., Holland, E. A., et al. (2018). Positive greetings at the door: Evaluation of a low-cost, high-yield proactive classroom management strategy. *Journal of Positive Behavior Interventions, 20*(3), 149–159.

Costa, A. L., & Kallick, B. (Eds.). (2000). *Activating and engaging habits of mind.* Alexandria, VA: ASCD.

Covey, S. R. (2004). *The 7 habits of highly effective people: Powerful lessons in personal change* (Revised ed.). New York: Free Press.

David, M. A. (2016). *Urban elementary teachers' perceptions of challenging behaviors and childhood trauma* [Master's thesis]. St. Paul, MN: St. Catherine University.

DeWolfe, D. J. (2000). *Training manual for mental health and human service workers in major disasters* (2nd ed.). Washington, DC: Center for Mental Health Services.

DuFour, R., DuFour, R., Eaker, R., Many, T., & Mattos, M. (2016). *Learning by doing: A handbook for Professional Learning Communities at Work* (3rd ed.). Bloomington, IN: Solution Tree Press.

Economist. (2009, June 19). *Joseph Juran.* Accessed at www.economist.com/node/13881008 on November 29, 2017.

Eller, J. F., & Eller, S. (2009). *Creative strategies to transform school culture.* Thousand Oaks, CA: Corwin Press.

Eller, J. F., & Hierck, T. (2021). *Trauma-sensitive instruction: Creating a safe and predictable classroom environment.* Bloomington, IN: Solution Tree Press.

Erickson, H. L. (2002). *Concept-based curriculum and instruction: Teaching beyond the facts.* Thousand Oaks, CA: Corwin Press.

Figley, C. R. (Ed.). (1995). *Compassion fatigue: Coping with secondary traumatic stress disorder in those who treat the traumatized.* New York: Routledge.

Fisher, D., & Frey, N. (2021). *Better learning through structured teaching: A framework for the gradual release of responsibility* (3rd ed.). Alexandria, VA: ASCD.

Forst, S. (2020). *The teacher's guide to self-care: Build resilience, avoid burnout, and bring a happier and healthier you to the classroom.* Chicago: The Designer Teacher LLC.

Fredrickson, B. L. (2009). *Positivity: Top-notch research reveals the 3-to-1 ratio that will change your life.* New York: Three Rivers Press.

Gage, N. A., & MacSuga-Gage, A. S. (2017). Salient classroom management skills: Finding the most effective skills to increase student engagement and decrease disruptions. *Report on Emotional and Behavioral Disorders in Youth, 17*(1), 13–18.

Gibbons, S., Murphy, D., & Joseph, S. (2011). Countertransference and positive growth in social workers. *Journal of Social Work Practice, 25*(1), 17–30. https://doi.org/10.1080/02650530903579246

Gillett, R. (2016). *18 teachers share what they wished they knew before they started teaching.* Accessed at www.businessinsider.com/what-teachers-wish-they-knew-before-they-started-teaching-2016-9 on September 10, 2023.

The Glossary of Education Reform. (2014). *Formative assessment.* Accessed at www.edglossary.org/formative-assessment on July 6, 2023.

Grant, A. (2013). *Give and take: A revolutionary approach to success.* New York: Viking.

Guskey, T. R. (2015). *On your mark: Challenging the conventions of grading and reporting.* Bloomington, IN: Solution Tree Press.

Guskey, T. R. (2023). *Implementing mastery learning* (3rd ed.). Thousand Oaks, CA: Corwin Press.

Guskey, T. R., & Bailey, J. M. (2010). *Developing standards-based report cards.* Thousand Oaks, CA: Corwin Press.

Hafızoğlu, A., & Yerdelen, S. (2019). The role of students' motivation in the relationship between perceived learning environment and achievement in science: A mediation analysis. *Science Education International, 30*(4), 251–260.

Hammond, Z. (2015). *Culturally responsive teaching and the brain: Promoting authentic engagement and rigor among culturally and linguistically diverse students.* Thousand Oaks, CA: Corwin.

Hierck, T. (2016). *Why assess?* Accessed at https://allthingsassessment.info/2016/02/25/why-assess on September 29, 2023.

Hierck, T. (2017). *Seven keys to a positive learning environment in your classroom.* Bloomington, IN: Solution Tree Press.

Hierck, T., & Freese, A. (2018). *Assessing unstoppable learning.* Bloomington, IN: Solution Tree Press.

Hierck, T., & Larson, G. (2018). *Grading for impact: Raising student achievement through a target-based assessment and learning system.* Thousand Oaks, CA: Corwin Press.

Hierck, T., & and Weber, C. (2023). *The road to success with MTSS: A ten-step process for schools.* Bloomington, IN: Solution Tree Press.

Hodge, A. (2020). *Mispronouncing your non-White students' names is a racist act.* Accessed at https://medium.com/@msalihodge/mispronouncing-your-non-white-students-names-is-a-racist-act-567dc33a8bdf on August 10, 12023.

Hughes, J. (Director). (1986). *Ferris Bueller's day off* [Film]. Hollywood, CA: Paramount Pictures.

Kajitani, A. (2022). *101 tips for teaching online: Helping students think, learn, and grow—no matter where they are!* Bloomington, IN: Solution Tree Press.

Kanold, T. D., & Boogren, T. H. (2022). *Educator wellness: A guide for sustaining physical, mental, emotional, and social well-being.* Bloomington, IN: Solution Tree Press.

Kenardy, J., De Young, A., Le Brocque, R., & March, S. (2011). *Childhood trauma reactions: A guide for teachers from preschool to year 12.* Brisbane, Queensland, Australia: CONROD Centre of National Research on Disability and Rehabilitation Medicine. Accessed at https://schools.aidr.org.au/media/4605/conrod_childhood-trauma-reactions.pdf.

Kise, J. A. G. (2021). *Doable differentiation: Twelve strategies to meet the needs of all learners.* Bloomington, IN: Solution Tree Press.

Kohn, A. (1999). *Punished by rewards: The trouble with gold stars, incentive plans, As, praise, and other bribes.* New York: Houghton Mifflin Harcourt.

Kruse, K. (2016). The 80/20 rule and how it can change your life. *Forbes*. Accessed at www .forbes.com/sites/kevinkruse/2016/03/07/80-20-rule/?sh=4074a8cb3814 on August 13, 2023.

Lally, P., van Jaarsveld, C. H. M., Potts, H. W. W., & Wardle, J. (2010). How are habits formed: Modeling habit formation in the real world. *European Journal of Social Psychology*, *40*(6), 998–1009.

Luster, R. (2021, September 30). *When life doesn't feel real anymore* [Blog post]. Accessed at www.psychologytoday.com/us/blog/more-feeling/202109/when-life-doesnt-feel-real -anymore on October 1, 2023.

Marsac, M. L., & Ragsdale, L. B. (2020). *Tips for recognizing, managing secondary traumatic stress in yourself*. Accessed at https://publications.aap.org/aapnews/news/14395/Tips-for -recognizing-managing-secondary-traumatic?autologincheck=redirected on September 29, 2023.

Maslow, A. H. (1943). A theory of human motivation. *Psychological Review*, *50*(4), 370–396.

McCarthy, J. (2018). *Extending the silence*. Accessed at www.edutopia.org/article/extending- silence on July 27, 2023.

McFarlane, L. (2023). *Why pronouncing student names correctly matters, and how to get them right*. Accessed at www.edweek.org/leadership/why-pronouncing-student-names-correctly -matters-and-how-to-get-them-right/2023/07 on September 29, 2023.

Meinecke, C. (2010, June 5). *Self-care in a toxic world*. Accessed at www.psychologytoday.com /us/blog/everybody-marries-the-wrong-person/201006/self-care-in-toxic-world on June 15, 2023.

Mendler, A. (2014). *"Why do we need to learn this?"* Accessed at www.edutopia.org/blog/why -do-we-need-to-learn-this-allen-mendler on September 11, 2023.

MindPeace. (2020). *Self-care guide*. Accessed at https://mindpeacecincinnati.com/wp-content /uploads/SelfCareGuide_July2020.pdf on July 6, 2023.

Moore, M. (2021, September 13). 10 things veteran teachers wish they knew as new teachers [Blog post]. *Primary Paradise*. Accessed at www.myprimaryparadise.com/2021/09/13 /veteran-advice-new-teachers on July 19, 2023.

Morin, A. (2015). *5 reasons studies say you have to choose your friends wisely*. Accessed at www .psychologytoday.com/us/blog/what-mentally-strong-people-dont-do/201504/5-reasons -studies-say-you-have-choose-your-friends on August 12, 2023.

Murphy, M. (Writer), & Einhorn, R. (Director). (2022, January 11). Wishlist (Season 1, Episode 3) [TV series episode]. In Werner Walian (Executive Producer), *Abbott Elementary*. Warner Bros. Television; 20th Television.

National Alliance on Mental Illness. (n.d.). *Self-care inventory*. Accessed at www.nami.org /NAMI/media/Extranet-Education/HF15AR6SelfCare.pdf on June 15, 2023.

National Child Traumatic Stress Network. (2008). *Self care for educators*. Accessed at www .nctsn.org/sites/default/files/resources/self_care_for_educators.pdf on October 1, 2023.

National Child Traumatic Stress Network. (2011). *Secondary traumatic stress: A fact sheet for child-serving professionals*. Los Angeles: Author.

Oliver, R., & Reschly, D. (2007). *Effective classroom management: Teacher preparation and professional development*. Accessed at https://files.eric.ed.gov/fulltext/ED543769.pdf on September 8, 2023.

Orchard, K., & Souers, K. (2020). *Culture of safety element 2 of 3: Predictability*. Accessed at www.fosteringresilientlearners.org/blog/2020/2/17/culture-of-safety-element-2-of-3 -predictable on July 19, 2023.

Pankonin, A., & Myers, R. (2017). *Teachers' use of positive and negative feedback: Implications for student behavior*. Accessed at https://wp.nyu.edu/steinhardt-appsych_opus/teachers-use-of -positive-and-negative-feedback-implications-for-student-behavior on August 12, 2023.

Queensland Program of Assistance to Survivors of Torture and Trauma. (2016). *Compassion fatigue, burnout and vicarious trauma: A Queensland Program of Assistance to Survivors of Torture and Trauma (QPASTT) guidebook*. Accessed at https://qpastt.org.au/wordpress /wp-content/uploads/2014/05/QPASTT-guide-compassion-fatigue-burnout-and-vicarious -trauma-FINAL.pdf on December 28, 2023.

Red Cross. (2014). *Program level registration guide—Red Cross Swim Kids*. Accessed at www .redcross.ca/crc/documents/What-We-Do/Swimming-Water-Safety/swimguide/tp_ws _registration_guide_rcsk_oct2014.pdf on September 29, 2023.

Rice, K. F., & Groves, B. M. (2005). *Hope and healing: A caregiver's guide to helping young children affected by trauma*. Washington, DC: Zero to Three Press.

Richter, E., Lazarides, R., & Richter, D. (2021). Four reasons for becoming a teacher educator: A large-scale study on teacher educators' motives and well-being. *Teaching and Teacher Education, 102*, Article 103322. https://doi.org/10.1016/j.tate.2021.103322

Roberto, M. (2021, April 9). *Engaging students on the first day and every day: 7 strategies for connecting in the classroom*. Harvard Business Publishing Education. Accessed at https:// hbsp.harvard.edu/inspiring-minds/engaging-students-on-the-first-day-and-every-day on February 22, 2023.

Rodrigues, P. F. S., & Pandeirada, J. N. S. (2018). When visual stimulation of the surrounding environment affects children's cognitive performance. *Journal of Experimental Child Psychology, 176*, 140–149.

Rojstaczer, S., & Healy, C. (2012). Where A is ordinary: The evolution of American college and university grading, 1940–2009. *Teachers College Record, 114*(7), 1–23.

Saakvitne, K. W., Pearlman, L. A., Traumatic Stress Institute, & Center for Adult and Adolescent Psychotherapy. (1996). *Transforming the pain: A workbook on vicarious traumatization*. New York: Norton.

Safe Schools New Orleans. (n.d.). *Teacher wellness and self-care*. Accessed at https:// safeschoolsnola.tulane.edu/teacher-wellness on July 6, 2023.

Sanders, R. (2013). *Researchers find out why some stress is good for you.* Accessed at https://news .berkeley.edu/2013/04/16/researchers-find-out-why-some-stress-is-good-for-you on July 28, 2023.

Smith, R., & Dearborn, G. (2016). *Conscious classroom management.* Accessed at www. consciousteaching.com/web/wp-content/uploads/CH-13.Breaking-Cycle.CCM_1.pdf on March 12, 2018.

Solution Tree. (n.d.). *Tina H. Boogren.* Accessed at www.solutiontree.com/tina-h-boogren.html on July 28, 2023.

Splevins, K. A., Cohen, K., Joseph, S., Murray, C., & Bowley, J. (2010). Vicarious posttraumatic growth among interpreters. *Qualitative Health Research, 20*(12), 1705–1716. https://doi.org/10.1177/1049732310377457

Stahnke, R., & Blömeke, S. (2021). *Novice and expert teachers' situation-specific skills regarding classroom management: What do they perceive, interpret and suggest?* Accessed at www. sciencedirect.com/science/article/abs/pii/S0742051X20314347?via%3Dihub on August 12, 2023.

Stiggins, R. (2004). Assessment, student confidence, and school success. *Phi Delta Kappan, 81*(3), 191–198.

Sue, D. W., Capodilupo, C. M., Torino, G. C., Bucceri, J. M., Holder, A. M. B., Nadal, K. L., Esquilin, M. (2007). Racial microaggressions in everyday life: Implications for clinical practice. *American Psychologist, 62*(4), 271–286.

Thomas, C. (n.d.). *Top ten things I wish I had known when I started teaching.* Accessed at www .nctm.org/conferences-and-Professional-Development/Tips-for-Teachers/Top-Ten-Things-I-Wish-I-Had-Known-When-I-Started-Teaching on September 10, 2023.

Thomas B. Fordham Institute. (2021). *Children learn best when they feel safe and valued.* Accessed at https://fordhaminstitute.org/national/commentary/children-learn-best-when -they-feel-safe-and-valued on July 19, 2023.

Vaish, A., Grossmann, T., & Woodward, A. (2008). Not all emotions are created equal: The negativity bias in social-emotional development. *Psychological Bulletin, 134*(3), 383–403.

Valcour, M. (2016). Beating burnout. *Harvard Business Review.* Accessed at https://hbr. org/2016/11/beating-burnout on July 5, 2023.

Waddell, K. J. (2018). *You do, we do, I do: A strategy for productive struggle.* Accessed at www .ascd.org/ascd-express/vol14/num11/you-do-we-do-i-do-a-strategy-for-productive-struggle .aspx on July 27, 2023.

Weir, P. (Director). (1989). *Dead poets society* [Film]. Burbank, CA: Touchstone Pictures.

Wenk, L. (2017). *The importance of engaging prior knowledge.* Accessed at https://sites .hampshire.edu/ctl/2017/09/14/the-importance-of-engaging-prior-knowledge on September 8, 2023.

Wilding, M. J. (2022). *5 different types of imposter syndrome (and 5 ways to battle each one).* Accessed at www.themuse.com/advice/5-different-types-of-imposter-syndrome-and-5-ways-to-battle-each-oneon July 5, 2023.

Williams, K. C., & Hierck, T. (2015). *Starting a movement: Building culture from the inside out in professional learning communities.* Bloomington, IN: Solution Tree Press.

Willingham, A. J. (2023). *What is Maslow's hierarchy of needs? A psychology theory, explained.* Accessed at www.cnn.com/world/maslows-hierarchy-of-needs-explained-wellness-cec/index.html on September 5, 2023.

Wolcott, G. (2019). *Significant 72: Unleashing the power of relationships in today's schools.* Oshkosh, WI: FIRST Educational Resources.

Wong, H., & Wong, R. (2013). *How to start class every day.* Accessed at www.teachers.net/wong/OCT13 on July 5, 2023.

Wong, H. K., & Wong, R. T. (2014). *The classroom management book.* Mountain View, CA: Harry K. Wong Publications.

Wong, H. K., & Wong, R. T. (2018). *The first days of school: How to be an effective teacher* (5th ed.). Mountain View, CA: Harry K. Wong Publications.

Wormeli, R. (2011, November 1). Redos and retakes done right. *Educational Leadership, 69*(3), 22–26. Accessed at www.ascd.org/publications/educational-leadership/nov11/vol69/num03/Redos-and-Retakes-Done-Right.aspx on June 16, 2023.

Zhao, X., Yang, Y., Han, G., & Zhang, Q. (2022). The impact of positive verbal rewards on organizational citizenship behavior—The mediating role of psychological ownership and affective commitment. *Frontiers in Psychology.* Accessed at www.ncbi.nlm.nih.gov/pmc/articles/PMC9122041 on July 19, 2023.

INDEX

NUMBERS

2 × 4 relationship-building activity, 26, 27. *See also* building student-teacher relationships

80/20 rule, 55

A

Abbott Elementary, 9

academic standards, 62

administrators, understanding when to send students, 55

agendas, 10–11

Allday, R. A., 31, 46

assessments

about, 69

final thoughts: mastery and outcomes, 79–80

formative assessment, sample protocol for developing a, 72

formative assessment, understanding the purpose of, 69–71

grading, understanding the purpose of, 73–75

offering second chances, 75–77

planning interventions driven by evidence, 77–79

stopping and checking for understanding and, 65–66

summative assessment and student mastery, understanding the purpose of, 71, 73

asset-based approach, 20

automaticity, 33, 50

B

behavior management

about, 45–46

classroom management and, 31

definition of, 46

directing, correcting, or connecting and, 51–53

discouraging inappropriate behaviors, 51–56

expectations and, 46–47

final thoughts: that one student, 56

knowing what to do when Plan A doesn't work, 53–54

parents and guardians and, 88

promoting appropriate behaviors, 46–51

recognizing when students need their own plan, 55–56

remembering trauma and the 254-day student, 49–50

understanding when to send students out of class, 55

Black, P., 69

Boogren, T. H., 95–96

Botsman, R., 17

breaking it down/chunking, 62

building a long-term career as an educator

about, 105

being reflective, 108–109

building your network, 106–107

defining or redefining success and, 106

money and, 106

professional learning and, 107–108

surrounding yourself with good people, 107

when we teach, we live forever, 109

building student-teacher relationships
about, 17–18
asking questions, 25–26
behavior management and, 45
being real/vulnerability, 26, 28
final thoughts: the moments that matter, 29
helping students build relationships with each other, 28–29
hidden relationships in the classroom and, 28
knowing students' DNA, 19–20
relationships with content and, 28
saying goodbye, 22
saying hello, 21–22
showing your stuff/realia, 25
storytelling and, 24–25
students' living situations and, 22–24
students' names and, 18–19
using what you know to build connections and further learning, 21
burnout, 100–101
Business Insider, 99

C

class rosters, 19
classroom management
about, 31–32
behavior management and, 45
determining necessary classroom procedures and routines, 33–38
final thoughts: everything matters, 43
imposter syndrome and, 32
projecting confidence, 41–43
teaching classroom procedures and routines, 38–41
classroom setup
about, 3
behavior management and, 45
final thoughts: ideas are everywhere, 15
materials and supplies and, 11–15
safety, cleanliness, and visibility and, 3–8
seating charts and, 8–9

thinking about what to put on the walls, 9–11
classwork, 11
cleanliness, 5–6
cognitive processing styles, 63, 64
Comer, J., 18
communication
boundaries and, 15
nonverbal communication, 42
parents' and guardians' preferred method of contact, 82–84
report cards and, 74
ten positive reasons to reach out to parents and guardians, 84
working with translators, 85
conferencing, 54. *See also* behavior management
confidence, projecting, 41–43
connections. *See also* relationships
connect approach and behavior management, 52
fostering relationships and connectedness, 96, 99
storytelling and, 24
use of term, 17
using what you know to build connections and further learning, 21
content, building relationships with, 28
correct approach and behavior management, 52
Costa, A., 59
custodians, building meaningful relationships with, 5–6

D

Dead Poets Society, 57
desks
arranging desks, 6–7
common seating arrangements, 7–8
organizing your own desk and personal space, 14–15
using a seating chart, 8–9
direct approach and behavior management, 52
direct instruction, 63

diversity and asset-based approaches, 20

dreams, needs, and abilities (DNA), 19–20, 21, 23

E

elements of an engaging lesson. *See also* lessons

about, 58–59

building on prior knowledge, 59–61

learning targets and, 61–63

real-world connections and, 64–65

stopping and checking for understanding and, 65–66

using a variety of teaching strategies, 63–64

Eller, J. F., 99

emergency situations, 38. *See also* safety

emotions, recognizing and controlling, 102–104

essential procedures. *See also* classroom management

about, 33

how class begins, 33–34

how class ends/dismissal, 36

how class quiets down, 34–35

how to ask for help or answer questions, 35

how to handle transitions, 36

exit tickets, 67

expectations

creating, 47

example classroom expectations, 48

promoting appropriate behaviors and, 46–47

transitions and, 36

wall displays and, 10

eye contact, 42–43

F

Five Sense Calming Strategy, 53–54. *See also* behavior management

flexibility, 63

food and additional procedures, 38

food insecurity, 23

formative assessments. *See also* assessments

definition of, 69

formative and summative assessment types, 73

sample protocol for developing, 72

understanding the purpose of, 69–71

Freese, A., 69

G

Give and Take: Why Helping Others Drives Our Success (Grant), 107

Glossary of Education Reform, The, 69

grading. *See also* assessments

key consideration for grading policy, 75

understanding the purpose of, 73–75

Grant, A., 107

greeting students

saying "goodbye," 22

saying "hello," 21–22

tips to thrive, 34

Groves, B., 49

gun-related violence, 4–5. *See also* safety

Guskey, T., 74

H

Hierck, T., 46–47, 69, 99

homework

key consideration for grading policy, 75

posted reminders about, 11

students' living situations and, 23

how can I build relationships with students. *See* building student-teacher relationships

how do I get my students to behave. *See* behavior management

how do I know when students have learned. *See* assessments

how do I plan and deliver engaging lessons. *See* lessons

how do I set up my classroom. *See* classroom setup

how do I take care of myself. *See* self-care

how do I work with parents and guardians. *See* parents and guardians, working with

how should I manage my classroom. *See* classroom management

humor
    imposter syndrome and, 32
    letting go and promoting appropriate
        behavior, 50–51

I

I do, we do, you do, 90–91
imposter syndrome, 32
introduction, 1–2

K

Kallick, B., 59

L

language
    and learning about students' living
        situations, 23
    and working with parents and guardians, 82
    and working with translators, 85
learning goals, 11
learning journals, 67
learning targets
    being clear about what students will learn,
        61–63
    key consideration for grading policy and, 75
    wall displays and, 11
lessons
    about, 57
    final thoughts: evolve, improve, and stay
        flexible, 67
    knowing the elements of an engaging lesson,
        58–66
    planning for how to wrap things up, 66–67
    telling a story and, 25
    understanding where engagement starts, 58
letting go, 50–51

M

Maslow's hierarchy of needs, 4
materials and supplies
    books and curricula and, 13

finding inspiration and other things that
    keep you going, 14
planning for, 11–15
start with what's there, 12
supply closet and, 12–13
teacher desk and personal space and, 14–15
technology and, 13–14
Meinecke, C., 95
microaggressions, 18
mistakes, 26
modeling, 46
money, 106

N

names, learning, 9, 18–19
note-taking procedures, 37

P

parents and guardians, working with
    about, 81
    asking parents and guardians for advice,
        87–89
    asking parents and guardians how they're
        doing, 89
    final thoughts: working together, 91
    finding parents' and guardians' preferred
        method of contact, 82–84
    giving parents and guardians some questions
        they can ask their child, 85–86
    giving students some questions they can ask
        at home, 86–87
    inviting parents and guardians in, 89–91
    remembering that parent, guardian, and
        family can mean different things, 82
    ten positive reasons to reach out to parents
        and guardians, 84
    think time, 90
    using the power of questioning, 84–89
Pareto principal, 55
peers and student relationships, 28, 28–29
pencils, procedures for sharpening, 35, 40
phones, 46

picture prediction, 60

please and thank you, 28

positivity ratio, 48–49

post it, say it, remember it, 62–63

post-traumatic stress disorder (PTSD), 99, 101

posture, 42

prior knowledge
  about, 59
  asking questions and, 59–60
  picture prediction and, 60
  "previously on," 61

procedures
  definition of, 33
  determining necessary classroom procedures and routines, 33–38
  discussing why the procedure is important, 39–40
  food, 38
  how class begins, 33–34
  how class ends/dismissal, 36
  how class quiets down, 34–35
  how to ask for help or answer questions, 35
  how to handle transitions, 36, 37
  restroom procedures, 37
  safety, 38
  teaching classroom procedures and routines to students, 38–41

professional learning, 107–108

projecting confidence, 41–43

Q

questions
  asking parents and guardians for advice, 87–89
  asking parents and guardians how they're doing, 89
  building student-teacher relationships and, 25–26
  giving parents and guardians some questions they can ask their child, 85–86
  giving students some questions they can ask at home, 86–87

prior knowledge and, 59–60
professional learning and, 108
stopping to check for understanding and, 66
using the power of questioning, 84–89

quieting down
  essential procedures, 34–35
  teaching classroom procedures and routines to students, 40

R

realia, 25

real-world connections, 64–65

reassessments, retakes, and redos. *See also* assessments
  example reassessment ticket, 78
  key consideration for grading policy, 75
  offering second chances, 75–77

relationships. *See also* building student-teacher relationships
  building meaningful relationships with custodians, 5–6
  building your network, 106–107
  foundational pillars for strong relationships, 17
  helping students build relationships with each other, 28–29
  hidden relationships, 28
  how do I work with parents and guardians. *See* parents and guardians, working with
  please and thank you, 28
  self-care and, 96, 99
  surrounding yourself with good people, 107

reminders posted on the wall, 11

report cards, 74. *See also* grading

response to intervention (RTI), 77–79

restroom procedures, 35, 37

Rice, K., 49

routines
  definition of, 33
  determining necessary classroom procedures and routines, 33–38
  teaching classroom procedures and routines to students, 38–41

S

safety
  classroom setup and, 4–5
  emergency situations and additional
      procedures, 38
  predictability and, 11
Schlechty, P., 58
seating arrangements. *See also* desks
  common seating arrangements, 7–8
  using a seating chart, 8–9
seating charts, 8–9
secondary (vicarious) transformation, 101–102
secondary traumatic stress (STS), 99, 100–101
self-care
  about, 93–94
  final thoughts: plan your self-care, 104
  fostering relationships and connectedness,
      96, 99
  managing your secondary traumatic stress,
      99–102
  recognizing and controlling your emotions,
      102–104
  self-care survey: starting point, 97–98
  six elements of, 94–95
  taking time for yourself, 95–96
  understanding your self-care options, 94–95
  when to stop, continue, or start, 104
stress. *See also* self-care
  managing your secondary traumatic stress,
      99–102
  stress responses, 93
student mastery, understanding the purpose of
      summative assessment and, 71, 73
students
  learning about students' living situations,
      22–24
  learning students' first names, 9
  pronouncing students' names correctly,
      18–19
  remembering trauma and the 254-day
      student, 49–50
substitute teacher procedures, 37

Sue, D., 18
summative assessments. *See also* assessments
  formative and summative assessment
      types, 73
  understanding the purpose of summative
      assessment and student mastery, 71, 73
supply closet, 12–13

T

Teagues, J., 9
technology
  materials and supplies, 13–14
  promoting appropriate behaviors and, 46
  technology use procedures, 37–38
think time, 90
Thomas, C., 65
time out/refocus, 54. *See also* behavior
      management
tips to thrive
  arranging desks, 7
  asking for help, 100
  building student relationships, 22
  communication and behavior, 56
  flexibility, 63
  greeting students, 34
  learning students' first names, 9
  professional learning, 108
  response to intervention (RTI), 79
  setting the tone for learning, 61
  technology, 14
  working with translators, 85
  wrap-up time, 67
transitions, 36, 37, 40
translators, 85
trauma
  definition of, 49
  managing your secondary traumatic stress,
      99–102
  remembering trauma and the 254-day
      student, 49–50
trust and relationships, 17, 26

V

Valcour, M., 99

verbal warnings, 54. *See also* behavior
    management

visibility, 6–8. *See also* classroom setup

vulnerability, 26, 28

W

wall decor

    devoting space to what is most important,
        10–11

    pointing things out, 11

    simplicity, 10

    thinking about what to put on the walls,
        9–11

Wenk, L., 59

Wiliam, D., 69

Wong, H., 31

Wong, R., 31

Wormeli, R., 75

Owning It
Alex Kajitani
Today's fast-changing culture presents a great challenge—and a great opportunity—in schools and in the teaching profession. With *Owning It*, you will discover an array of easy-to-implement strategies designed to help you excel in your classroom, at your school, and in your community.
BKF835

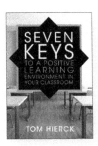

Seven Keys to a Positive Learning Environment in Your Classroom
Tom Hierck
Creating a positive classroom learning environment is a complex but necessary task. By following the seven keys the author outlines, teachers can establish clearer expectations, enhance instruction and assessment practices, and foster quality relationships with students, maximizing the potential of all students.
BKF721

Thriving as a New Teacher
John F. Eller and Sheila A. Eller
Discover strategies and tools for new-teacher success. Explore the six critical areas related to teaching that most impact new teachers and their students, from understanding yourself and implementing effective assessments to working confidently and effectively with colleagues.
BKF661

The Beginning Teacher's Field Guide
Tina H. Boogren
The joys and pains of starting a teaching career often go undiscussed. This guide explores the personal side of teaching, offering crucial advice and support. The author details six phases every new teacher goes through and outlines classroom strategies and self-care practices.
BKF806

Solution Tree | Press   *a division of* Solution Tree

Visit SolutionTree.com or call 800.733.6786 to order.